"Cyprian Consiglio is a very contemporary monk, who believes that the call to contemplation is universal and sees the current interest in Eastern spirituality as an incentive to seek the way of interiority within the Christian tradition. This approach must be greeted with delight, particularly as he brings with him the words of such as Origen, Bede Griffiths, Sri Aurobindo, Swami Abhishiktananda, and Simone Weil, and supports his arguments with wisdom from the Fourth Gospel, the Upanishads, Buddhism, and Taoism. A cornucopia of richness and delight and a fitting book for our time."

> —Shirley du Boulay
> Author of *Beyond the Darkness:*
> *A Biography of Bede Griffiths* and *The Cave of the Heart:*
> *The Life of Swami Abhishiktananda*

"It's not easy to talk about the Christian mystical tradition in universal terms without resorting to syncretism, but in *Prayer in the Cave of the Heart*, Camaldolese monk Cyprian Consiglio takes on the challenge with great love and shining integrity. *Prayer in the Cave of the Heart* is clearly the fruit of serious scholarly inquiry, courageous pilgrimage, and a humble, disciplined life of unceasing prayer. In this invitingly simple but richly packed guide to the Christian via negativa, Consiglio holds out the hope that we, too, can find our way through the narrow gate that leads to contemplation."

> —Paula Huston
> Author of *Forgiveness: Following Jesus into Radical Loving*

PRAYER IN THE CAVE OF THE HEART

THE UNIVERSAL CALL TO CONTEMPLATION

Cyprian Consiglio

LITURGICAL PRESS
Collegeville, Minnesota

www.litpress.org

Library of Congress Cataloging-in-Publication Data

Consiglio, Cyprian.
    Prayer in the cave of the heart : the universal call to contemplation
/ Cyprian Consiglio.
        p. cm.
    Includes bibliographical references.
    ISBN 9780814632765
  1. Prayer—Christianity.   I. Title.
    BV210.3.C655 2009
    248.3'2—dc22   2009024453

CONTENTS

PREFACE

The most important thing is to find peace and share it with others.

—Thich Nhat Hahn

It is important for me to say right at the beginning that I write this for you perhaps as a teacher, or even better as a fellow student, but not as any kind of guru or master. (Actually, I like to think of myself as someone who took really good notes in class and is sharing them with all his friends!)

During the first few years of my monastic life, from time to time I would go home to Arizona, where I had been living for some years before joining the monastery, and tell people that I felt as if I had "finally discovered the Good News!" I remember giving a conference once to young people and trying to explain to them what I thought I had learned, but my words fell flat. I had no way of being able to articulate what I thought I had learned, and the fact was that I had made only my own first baby steps in the way myself. Now, after some years of monastic life and regular practice, and after having written my master's thesis on contemplative anthropology and devouring as many books as possible from as many different traditions as possible, I am beginning to have a little bit of a vocabulary. And it is from that that I share these thoughts with you.

We sometimes speak of the monastery and particularly of the monastic cell as a laboratory, a place where some people are granted the luxury of making the interior journey, of living the contemplative life. More and more, however, monks are coming to understand that it is their obligation to share the fruits of that journey with others. It was at one time thought—and often still is today—that what monasticism really has to offer is a type of learning that is rooted in a wisdom tradition; or a certain style of liturgical celebration that is formal and interior in style; or a certain way of living that is simpler, more sober, and more focused than that found outside the monastery. But we must understand that this type of learning, this type of prayer, and this style of life *come from* the contemplative life as much as they are meant to lead to it; they *come from* an experience of the God of love as the center of one's being as much as they are meant to lead to it.

In other words, none of these "monastic" elements is an end in itself. I myself, for example, have engaged in teaching liturgy, preaching, and giving missions, in addition to the work that I have done and still do in music—composing, recording, and giving concerts. But, since entering monastic life, I have come to realize that none of these things, important though they may be, is at the heart of what I am about. If I start to feel myself getting too caught up in liturgy for the sake of liturgy, or music for the sake of music, or preaching for the sake of preaching, I know that I am not living my essential vocation. Liturgy, music, preaching—other people can do these things. I am a monk, and I am called to spread the Good News in whatever work I do. My expertise is not in social justice; it is not really in academics and certainly not in parish administration. Anything I say, teach, write, or do must be, essentially and ultimately, about trying to convey and lead people to an experience of interiority, an experience of the indwelling presence of God. To paraphrase Abhishiktananda:

> If monks open their mouths
> it will normally only be to speak about the inner Mystery
> and how to discover it hidden as it is in the depths of the heart.
> They will steadfastly avoid all purely intellectual discussions;
> not for them are the conferences and seminars of the learned,
> or even the gathering of sages.
> But they will never refuse to help humble and genuine seekers,
> those who are truly eager to know God,
> and will show them the way to the cave of the heart.[1]

It has become more and more clear that, aside from their very presence, silent as it may be, monks and contemplatives are called to share with the world and the church today the way of contemplative prayer, the way of meditation. It is the main gift that they have to offer. This is what I have learned from monks such as Abhishiktananda, Bede Griffiths, Thomas Merton, John Main, and Laurence Freeman, along with Thomas Keating and Basil Pennington. I have also been influenced by many others, Carmelites such as Ruth Burrows and William MacNamara, and Jesuits such as William Johnson and Heinrich Dumoulin. My insights have perhaps been most deeply shaped by the desert monastics: Antony the Great, who heard the Gospel proclaimed, "Go sell everything you have and give it to the poor, and come and follow me," and took that as a call to go into the wilderness, to live in tombs and battle the demons and seek purity of heart; and Evagrius of Pontus, who turned that same biblical injunction around to say, "Go sell everything you have and give it to the poor so that you may *pray without ceasing*."

And so, what I aim to do for and with you in the pages that follow is to share something of what I have learned through the monastic tradition and practice about meditation and contemplative prayer, and to give you the opportunity to pursue the practice yourself.

Where This Began

In 2004, toward the beginning of this particular phase in my own life, when I was given permission to live on my own away from my monastic community and engage in apostolic work, I filled in at a parish for a classmate of mine in Santa Cruz, California, while he was on sabbatical. During that time some of the parishioners asked me to lead a series on prayer and meditation. I could hardly refuse, though I felt daunted by the task of once again trying to articulate what I had begun to learn. My conditions for agreeing to do the series were that it be open to people of all faiths; that we hold the conferences in the hall, which would make it easier for people who might not feel comfortable inside a church to attend; and that I be allowed to draw from the various traditions I had studied outside of Judeo-Christianity so that I could share with others what I myself was beginning to discover: that the call to contemplation is universal, that there are resonances between the mystical traditions of the East and the Christian mystical tradition—a tradition of which many people are unaware and which is accessible to all.

I set myself to the task in a sort of flow, beginning with the very basics—the "what" and "why"—and then naturally moving on to follow a somewhat historical approach to the Christian contemplative experience as I understood it: prayer of the heart in the teachings of Jesus, in the writings of St. Paul, in the desert monastic tradition, in the Carmelite tradition, in the Eastern Christian and Orthodox tradition. While preparing the original talks, I was amazed both at what pleasure I was taking in writing them and at how, quite often, I would remember a quote or some kernel of wisdom from a book I had read a decade or so earlier in the hope of being able to share it with someone someday, and at how I could often go right back to that book and find the reference with little trouble. It was as if I had been granted the luxury of space and time to read all those books solely for the purpose of being able to distill the teaching contained in them, practice what they taught, and then pass it on to others.

Happily, the series on prayer and meditation was a great success, drawing more than a hundred people each week. It culminated in an inter-religious meditation vigil for peace on New Year's Eve. It also spawned a number of smaller groups determined to continue and deepen the learning and practice. In the years since then I have been asked to present the same series or give talks on the subject in many different locations.

The chapters of this book are modeled on the sessions in the original series, compiled and edited after much urging that I put down something in writing. My hope, of course, is that this book may have the same effect on you that the original sessions had on those who participated in them, that it may stimulate in you a desire to pray and meditate, to grow closer to the Divine through the interior way, both for the healing of your own body, soul, and spirit and for that of others in this world most in need of this mercy.

One final word: all of this is mere verbiage without a commitment to daily practice. I have come to know that spirituality is eminently a practical science—it concerns what we do when we get up in the morning, how we spend our day, how we go to bed at night—and specifically how much time and energy we are willing to dedicate to the practice of prayer and meditation. So, although each chapter in this book addresses some aspect of the way of meditation, making use of sources from both the Western and Eastern traditions, each chapter also includes practical considerations regarding questions of method.

The most basic practice of all is simply that of making time to pray. It is commonly recommended that one dedicate to the practice of meditation two periods of the day, hopefully in roughly the same place and at the same time—once in the morning and once in the evening. Probably a realistic goal for most people is twenty minutes at each sitting, but even that length of time can be a daunting goal at first. So, if it begins as a matter of five minutes, increasing slowly to six, ten, fifteen, let it be so. As the old monastic adage states, "Pray as you can, not as you can't!"

With this as our starting point, let us begin our journey into the cave of the heart.

1

THE UNIVERSAL CALL
TO CONTEMPLATION

The wise withdrew the senses from the world of change
and, seeking immortality,
looked within and beheld the deathless Self.

—Katha Upanishad

Do you not know that you are God's temple,
and that God's Spirit dwells in you?

—1 Corinthians 3:16

There is such a hunger for interiority in our world, in our culture. I am convinced that this is why ashrams and *zendos* and yoga centers are full, because people—often Christians—are finding there a way of interiority and a sense of their own selves as vessels of divinity. These are things that Christian preachers and teachers have apparently not been able to convey, perhaps that Christian preachers and teachers have not yet understood themselves.

The way of meditation and contemplation is necessarily an interior way, and the interior way goes against our grain as human beings. I often like to think of it as swimming upstream. The *Katha Upanishad* of the Indian tradition says

> The self-existent Lord pierced the senses to turn outward.
> Thus we look to the world outside
> and see not the Self [or "spirit"; literally *"atman"*] within us.
> The wise withdrew the senses from the world of change
> and, seeking immortality,
> looked within and beheld the deathless Self.[1]

1

God made us human beings so that our senses turn outward. This is why, at least through our first years of life (and for some people through all of their lives), we tend to spend most of our time looking outward at the world of sense objects and never even think to look into ourselves. Now and then some daring souls who are unsatisfied, who are longing for that which survives death and decay and change, venture to look inside, and when they do they find themselves, their real selves, the true self, which, as St. Paul says, is "hidden with Christ in God" (Col 3:3).

There are a few monks I will refer to with some frequency in the pages ahead; one of them, whose words I quoted in the preface, is Abhishiktananda. This was his Indian name; his given name was Henri le Saux and he was a French Benedictine monk who moved to India in 1945 after having spent eighteen years at the Abbey of St. Anne de Kergonan in France. With another Frenchman, a priest named Jules Monchanin, le Saux founded Saccidananda Ashram, Shantivanam, in southern India. He would later move to an area near the source of the Ganges in northern India and become an itinerant monk, a deep contemplative, a Hindu-Christian *sannyasi*, or renunciant.[2] Abhishiktananda wrote many books—including a famous book called *Prayer*—that incorporate what he learned from the experience of having immersed himself in Indian thought and practice. The essence of his personal journey is reflected in the title of his published diaries, *Ascent to the Depth of the Heart*. To arrive at the Ganges, the source, one must climb high into the Himalayas. This pilgrimage is an apt metaphor for the interior way: we go up to the source, which is really the fount that flows from within. We ascend to the depths or, as Gregory of Nyssa put it in his writings on humility, we "descend to the heights."[3]

An Interior Way: The Gift of the East

Often I have heard it said that the difference between an Asian and a Westerner is shown most clearly by the answer to a simple question. Ask Westerners where God is and they will point to the sky, or all around them, or to some specific place outside them. I remember once visiting a seminary where a young deacon was giving the homily at Vespers, which also included Benediction of the Blessed Sacrament. The young man was preaching with great intensity. "You ask where God is? Do you want to know where God is? I'll tell you where God is! God is right there!" he said, pointing to the tabernacle. "That's where God is!"

Now, I would never deny that God is in the tabernacle, because I believe in the real presence of Jesus in the Eucharist. But if you were to ask an Asian where God is, chances are that the person would first of all point to his or her own heart. While pondering such a response, we might also want to consider this: a good Catholic, after having participated in the eucharistic celebration and having received the sacrament, could just as easily point to his or her own belly as to the tabernacle and say, "Here is where God is!" Or any Christian could quote St. Paul or St. Peter, who in their letters speak of the believer as being "God's dwelling" or "a living temple." Still, looking inward would generally not be our first response as Westerners.

Carl Jung wrote that the strange antithesis between East and West is expressed most clearly in religious practice. We Westerners, he says, "speak of religious uplift and exaltation; for us God is the Lord of the universe, we have a religion of brotherly love, and in our heaven-aspiring churches there is a *high altar*." On the other hand, the Indian, for example, "speaks of *dhyana*, of self-immersion, and of *sinking* into meditation; God is within all things" and especially within the human person. There is a certain turning away from the outer world to the inner world. Jung offers as an example the old Indian temples in which the altar is sunk six to eight feet deep in the earth. "We believe in doing," he writes, while "the Indian in passive *being*. Our religious exercises consist of prayer, worship, and singing hymns. The Indian's most important exercise is yoga, an immersion in what we would call an unconscious state, but which [an Indian] praises as the highest consciousness." He goes on to note that "yoga is the most eloquent expression of the Indian mind and at the same time the instrument continually used to produce this particular attitude of mind."[4]

Just as we distinguish between the interior way and the exterior way, God experienced outside as opposed to God experienced within, we also distinguish between the prophetic religions, those that meet God in history, and the mystical ones, in which the path to union with God is through interiority. There is, to be sure, actually even a kind of suspicion—perhaps a healthy one!—in the Christian West about terms such as "mystical," just as there is a criticism leveled against Westerners at times for being too focused on externals.

At this point I would like to introduce another monk whom I will be quoting frequently, Bede Griffiths, an Oxford-educated English Benedictine monk who went to India in 1955. After a short-lived monastic experiment in Bangalore and helping to found another Christian monastic community in Kerala named Kurisamala, he went on to assume responsibility for Shantivanam from Abhishiktananda and turned it into an important place of pilgrimage for people from all over the world, while he himself became a prominent figure in the area of inter-religious dialogue.

Here is how Bede Griffiths explains the difference—and the relationship—between the Western and Eastern approaches:

> The Semitic religions, Judaism and Islam, reveal the transcendent aspect of the divine Mystery with incomparable power. The oriental religions reveal the divine Immanence with immeasurable depth. Yet in each the opposite aspect is contained, though in a more hidden way. We have to discover the inner relationship between these different aspects of Truth and unite them in ourselves.[5]

Carl Jung similarly wrote that "the Holy Spirit's task and charge" is to "reconcile and reunite the opposites in the human individual through a special development of the human soul."[6] Could not this gift of interiority from the East help us reconcile and reunite the opposites within each of us and further develop our souls?

I want to make clear that I am suggesting not that Christians need to be Buddhists or Hindus, but that we may have reached a point in our spiritual evolution when our own gifts might need to be complemented by the contemplative gifts of these cultures. William Johnston, who is perhaps the *grandpère* of all these things, quotes "the saintly Jewish mystic" Simone Weil, who, he says, spoke "prophetically of Europe's need" for Eastern spirituality:

It seems that Europe requires genuine contacts with the East in order to remain spiritually alive. It is also true that there is something in Europe which opposes the Oriental spirit, something specifically Western . . . and we are in danger of being devoured by it.

And then Johnston goes on to ask,

What is this specifically Western thing that opposes the East and could devour the European soul? Is it rationalism, materialism, legalism, intolerance, arrogance, and all those vices that Paul attributes to the ungodly in the Epistle to the Romans? Be that as it may, the world today needs the spirituality of Asia. Western Christianity is not enough. We need Eastern mysticism to help us penetrate more deeply into the Gospel of Jesus Christ. Now more than ever the world cries out for wise men and women from the East, people who will follow the star bringing gifts of gold, incense and myrrh to the child who has been born.[7]

Jung himself once pointed out that life seems to have gone out of the churches in the West, and as its next dwelling place the Holy Spirit appears to have selected the human individual. This should come as no surprise to us Christians. "Destroy this temple," said Jesus, "and in three days I will raise it up" (John 2:19). John tells us that Jesus was talking about the temple of his own body. But by extension he was also speaking about the temples of our own bodies. St. Paul asks, "Do you not know that you are God's temple and that God's Spirit dwells in you?" (1 Cor 3:16) and then goes on to state unequivocally, "For God's temple is holy, and you are that temple" (1 Cor 3:17).

Over the past few decades we in the West have seriously begun to appreciate the "other half of our soul" as it has been revealed to us by Asia. This is not to say that we have not had our own gifts to offer as well. It has been Western Christians who, spurred on by the message of the Gospel, have consistently and reliably responded to natural disasters in foreign countries, who have built missionary hospitals and orphanages and have fought for political and social advances throughout the world. I know of Buddhists and Hindus who see this—a commitment to social engagement and a talent for organizational genius—as the gift of Christianity to their traditions.

The structure of Western monasticism was undoubtedly influential in the Hindu monastic revival of the nineteenth century; Mahatma Gandhi was greatly influenced by the Beatitudes in his involvement with the plight of his people; Buddhists speak openly about "socially engaged Buddhism" and credit this to the influence of Western Christianity. Ours is an age of complementarity, of reciprocity, a coming together of East and West in many ways.

The Universal Call to Contemplation

The one and only time that I personally met Fr. Bede Griffiths and heard him speak, the title of the talk he gave was "The Universal Call to Contemplation." This was the underlying theme of all of his teaching. It has become a central core of my own teaching as well, and is foundational to everything that follows.

I understand this "universal call" first of all to mean that everyone is called to share in the grace of the contemplative life. It is for people in all walks of life, not just for monks and nuns and "professional religious." This, as was mentioned at the beginning of this chapter, is something that people are discovering through immersing themselves in other traditions. It is the reason why *zendos* and ashrams and yoga centers are full.

Some years ago, for example, I had a suspicion that there were many Christians who had left Christianity for a non-Christian Eastern tradition, having found in that tradition something really valuable, namely, a way of meditation and interiority in general. It was not that they had wanted to leave their religion of birth behind; it was that they simply could not find their way home again. Having discovered a profound sense of contemplative presence through the practice of Zen meditation or yoga, they might then have experienced Christian liturgies and homilies as banal and any practical application of spirituality to daily life—through diet, ecology, care of the body, healthy interpersonal skills—as sadly lacking in their Christian community. Perhaps they had tried to speak with their parish priest or religious education coordinator of what they had discovered, only to be dismissed with a look of utter incomprehension or with rolled eyes. Conversely, I sensed that there might be Christians who had entered the church after a history with one of these other traditions, people who had never been able to find a way to reconcile these things with their new-found Christianity and assumed that they had to be left behind. Many of these people seemed to have no idea that there was also a Christian contemplative tradition that was accessible to all.

My suspicion was confirmed when I began giving talks and leading programs on prayer and meditation. In preparing my presentations, I specifically decided to follow the line of thinking used by Bede Griffiths, to teach about the Christian contemplative tradition while always keeping an eye on the universal contemplative tradition, drawing as many analogies and comparisons (negative and positive) as possible from other traditions. The result was that, again and again, people would respond by expressing the same sentiment: "I have studied yoga (or *zazen* or TM or *vipassana*) for years and I never knew how to tie it in with my Christianity; I never knew that I could do it as a Christian, that there could be any connection between it and Christianity."

The call to contemplation is universal. People all over are hearing it, sensing it, receiving it, yearning for "something more," longing to go deeper, and looking for a new language with which to rearticulate ancient truths. The exodus to the East and Eastern practices has become for us a spur, an incentive to uncover our own contemplative tradition, to seek the way of interiority within our own tradition.

I stress this because there was a time in the church when the way of contemplative prayer was considered so esoteric that it belonged only to a certain elite few. I was told more than one story of how, in certain religious formation houses and monasteries, the writings of St. John of the Cross, for example, were kept under lock and key. Even monks and other religious were discouraged from seeking the way of pure prayer. And if one did get to crack open those books, one could easily get a sense that it was a pathway that was very ascetical and individualistic, a pathway that seemed to exclude ordinary people from contemplation.

The second meaning of this "universal call to contemplation" is that we discover in our own contemplative tradition a commonality with many other spiritual traditions that are not Judeo-Christian. Why? Simply put, because the source and the summit of all authentic spiritual traditions is the experience of union with God. When we stay close to this experience—both before and after it has been expressed and defined in ritual, dogma, or doctrine—we find much more in common than we might have anticipated. An openness to these other traditions might be able to help us rediscover or rearticulate our own truths in a way that might never have occurred to us. This openness could help us illuminate and appreciate in a new way some aspect of our own tradition that has not yet been fully formed in our own awareness or for which we have until now lacked an adequate vocabulary.

Universal Wisdom: The Bridge

There is such a sense of relief when people who have left Christianity for another contemplative tradition discover not only that Christianity has its own mystical tradition and its own mystical understanding of the Gospel but also that they can integrate into their Christianity the treasure they have found in the other tradition.

One of the most significant contributions that Bede Griffiths made to monastic spirituality was introducing the practice of doing *lectio divina*—holy reading—with texts from sacred traditions other than our own. Toward the end of his life he even compiled an anthology of those texts under the title *Universal Wisdom*. He believed, as I have come to believe, that there is much to be gleaned from reading others' descriptions of their experience of the Divine. It just could be that someone from another tradition will be able to express some aspect of the interior journey in a way that might not occur to us and that could spark in us either a sense of connection with or a thirst for that same experience.

As my brothers and sisters at Shantivanam Benedictine Ashram and many other ashrams in India do, my friends and I always begin our sessions with a reading from universal wisdom. In the same spirit, we will begin each chapter of this book with a brief quotation from the sacred texts of one of the great Eastern traditions as well as with a quotation from the Judeo-Christian scriptures. In addition to setting the theme of each chapter, these epigraphs are meant to serve as bridges—and we all know that bridges go two ways. They not only can help us understand someone else's tradition in a new light; they may also be able to help those from another tradition understand Christianity in a new light as they find in the Christian tradition resonances of their own spiritual theology.

We would do well to keep in mind that we Christians have our own Eastern tradition, the tradition of Byzantine Christianity, which stretches from the Fathers of the early Church and the desert monks all the way to the inspired teachers of today, such as Kallistos Ware and Antony Bloom, a tradition that has produced such classic texts as the *Philokalia* and *The Way of the Pilgrim*. In recent decades many Western Christians have begun to uncover the riches that are hidden in Byzantine Christianity, through music and liturgy, through iconography and literature, and, most important, through the contemplative tradition and the practice of the Jesus Prayer.

The Issue of Language

While space does not permit detailed treatment of the subject here, the issue of using terminology other than that rooted in Greek philosophical and Roman legal language is quite apropos of our discussion, especially with regard to authors such as Abhishiktananda, Bede Griffiths, William Johnson, John Main and some of the others I will cite in the pages ahead.

The original inspiration for Christianity is Jesus, who articulated his experience according to his own background—that of a Palestinian Jew steeped in the Torah, the Law and the Prophets, and the language of the psalms—and the background of his listeners. By the time the *kerygma* (i.e., the "proclamation" of the Good News) first began to be set down in writing, some thirty years had passed since the death and resurrection of Jesus. The story was the same, but the form of its telling was to a certain degree being shaped by the author, his circumstances, and his community. Certainly each of the Gospel writers had a particular audience in mind—Matthew's community was made up largely of Jewish converts, for example, while Luke was writing mainly for Gentiles. St. Paul borrowed from many sources to try to articulate the Gospel, particularly to people who had been steeped in Hellenistic thought, both Gentiles and Jews of the diaspora. This added another level of interpretation, a new set of terms for trying to describe the initial Gospel experience. And certainly by the second and third centuries, from the Neoplatonic period onward, yet another philosophical and epistemological layer was being added to the Gospel *kerygma* in an attempt to convey the mystical heart of the experience to a whole new generation of thinkers. Greek philosophical language (just like Roman law!) was to become so wedded to Christian theology that we could tend to think of it as canonical, inspired at the same level of authority as scripture itself. But many scholars have argued that it is not, and that such language is not essential to the inner meaning of the Gospel or to the experience of adoption that Jesus offers.

Now, what thinkers such as Abhishiktananda and Bede Griffiths asked was: what if Christianity were to be interpreted and passed on using the language of the Vedanta (an orthodox system of Hindu philosophy), the language of Mahayana Buddhism, or the language of Taoism or Confucian philosophy? Is it possible to take our experience of the Gospel and the Christian tradition and try to articulate it using non-Western philosophical or mystical language? The fact that we have not done this may perhaps account for the failure of missionary efforts in the Orient, Bede Griffiths says, especially in India, where we have used a philosophical language that makes little sense to the Indian mind. We have so often tried to pass on Greek terms and Roman culture (hence the Roman Rite of the Mass and Gregorian chant) instead of allowing the seed of the *kerygma* to take root in native philosophical and cultural soil, recognizing that the spark of the Divine and the inspiration of the Holy Spirit have been at work in other traditions as well.

At the same time, I think we have learned not to expect, much less desire, any easy kind of agreement, what one of my teachers called a "soggy syncretism," so as to say, "See, we are all the same." No, we are not all the same, and we disagree on some very fundamental things. I, for example, do not believe in reincarnation. It is not that I do not understand it; I think I do understand it. It is simply that I do not think that that is the way the universe operates. I also do not agree with what many of my Buddhist friends mean when they say that "there is no self."

For all of his searching into the common truth that underlies all religion, Bede Griffiths was the first to admit this.

> The Buddhist *nirvana* and the Hindu *moksha* are not the same, nor are they the same as the Christian vision of God. So the Buddhist, the Hindu, the Muslim and the Christian are all experiencing the ultimate Reality but experiencing it in different ways through their own love and through their own traditions of faith and knowledge. . . . There is a tendency to say that when one reaches the supreme state everything is the same and that there are no differences any more, but I do not think that is true.[8]

He goes on to say that, in a sense, "the experience of ultimate truth is different for each person, since each person is a unique image of God, a unique reflection of the one eternal light and love."[9]

And yet, in spite of these differences, there is still something that unites us—and it is not simply our quest for answers to the ultimate questions. More often than not it is some kind of an experience of the Divine, Ultimate Reality, the Source of Being, that has inspired the original movement. It seems to me undeniable that the ancient *rishis* (divinely inspired Hindu poets or sages; seers) and yogis of India, and the Buddha himself after sitting in meditation under the *bodhi* tree, and many of his followers, and the Sufi mystics, had very real and profound mystical experiences. When we read what they had to say—we who have had some experience of meditation and contemplation, some experience of the love of God poured into our hearts—we recognize in their words something of what we ourselves have known and perhaps have not been able to articulate.

Concerning Techniques

Many of the techniques that I will be discussing in the pages that follow have been drawn from other traditions, especially the traditions of Asia. In the "Letter to the Bishops of the Catholic Church on Some Aspects of Christian Meditation," issued by the Congregation for the Doctrine of the Faith in 1989, we find the following statement in chapter 5 on "Questions of Method": "The majority of the great religions which have sought union with God in prayer have also pointed out ways to achieve it."[10] The document then goes on to quote *Nostra Aetate*, the Second Vatican Council's declaration on relations with other religions:

> Just as "the Catholic church rejects nothing of what is true and holy in these religions,"[11] neither should these ways be rejected out of hand simply because they are not Christian. On the contrary, one can take from them what is useful so long as the Christian conception of prayer, its logic and requirements are never obscured. It is within the context of all of this that these bits and pieces should be taken up and expressed anew.[12]

Our aim here is to learn from other traditions "what is useful," while remaining faithful to and exploring ever more deeply the "Christian conception of prayer," which may actually appear clearer to us as we explore some of these techniques.

At the same time, the West has always had a suspicion with regard to technique—and perhaps with good reason. It is possible to become obsessed with technique and lose sight of the working of grace, of God's initiative. Prayer is not "magic." Awareness of this is inherent in and fundamental to the Christian concept of prayer. (It is not totally absent in other traditions either.) In other words, we do not conjure up God, we do not bring God down from heaven, and we do not make ourselves holy. We dispose ourselves, we stop, we listen, we wait, we watch, we make ourselves available, and we put ourselves in situations and environments that are conducive to prayer and meditation. And then we wait for the working of grace, like the bride awaiting the bridegroom.

Spirit, Soul, and Body: An Anthropology

Before we begin to address the topic of meditation proper, there is one other element I would like to introduce, and that is my understanding of the make-up of the human person, an understanding that will undergird all the reflections that follow. Like Bede Griffiths, I assume that the human person is made up not just of body and soul, but of body, soul, and spirit. You may think that this sounds more like an introduction to Christian anthropology than to Christian meditation, and you would not be far from the truth in thinking so. The famous maxim that dictates liturgical thought applies here as well: *Lex orandi, lex credendi.* Translated simply, this means, "The law of prayer is the law of belief." Translated even more colloquially, it means "How we pray is how we believe"— and vice versa! The fact is that all of our theological questions are also anthropological questions. Who we think we are, who we think God is, and what we think of the relationship between ourselves and God—each of these is crucial to our prayer life.

Generally in the West, and certainly in Western Christianity, we speak of the human person as being composed of either body and soul or body and spirit, though sometimes we do speak of the "spiritual soul."[13] Bede Griffiths, among others, found this anthropology lacking, and insisted that the human person is made up of body, soul, and spirit. Here is how he put it:

> We have a body, a physical organism, which is part of the physical organism of nature, and we have a soul, a *psyche*, which is a psychological organism, with its different faculties. But beyond both body and soul we are spirit, *pneuma* in Greek [*ruah* in Hebrew], *atman* in Sanskrit, and this is our point of union with the divine spirit. St. Francis de Sales calls this spirit the "fine point" of the soul. It is the point at which the human spirit is in touch with the Spirit of God. . . . Most people think of the human being as a body-soul, a psychological-physical organism, and have lost sight of the spirit, the point of human transcendence, which opens us both to God, the eternal Spirit, and to our fellow human beings. For it is at this depth of our being that we are in communion with one another. In our bodies and our souls we are all different and divided, but at this point of the spirit we are in communion with God and with one another.[14]

The Italian scholar Marco Vannini speaks beautifully of the human person thus:

Sarx, psyche, pneuma: body, soul, spirit. This was the ancient anthropology, and also the Christian anthropology. Having forgotten it means to have lost the experience of the spirit. Only when Christianity grew rigid in a dogmatic synthesis did it lose—of necessity—the spirit (or indeed confined it to the "supernatural") and create a body-soul bi-partite anthropology.[15]

In one of the last presentations of his life, Bede Griffiths said, "The body, mind, and spirit are the main focus of all my thinking presently; we have to integrate these three levels of reality that exist at every moment."[16] This view is echoed in the work of a writer greatly admired by Fr. Bede, Ken Wilber, who refers to an "integral spirituality." It is also a view that shaped the thought of the great Indian philosopher Sri Aurobindo, whose teachings on integral yoga had an important influence on Fr. Bede.

What is integral spirituality? Ken Wilber offers a concrete example in suggesting that a contemplative monk might perhaps have to supplement his practice with *hatha* yoga, weight training, therapy, and some kind of community service, so that he has a well-rounded life.[17] This applies not just to religious, but also to "church folks" in general who often have such a mistrust of the body and physicality. Actually, it applies to everyone, especially in our "information age," when so many of us find ourselves stuck behind computer screens and cut off from nature, eating food out of little plastic boxes and constantly bombarded with stimuli from TV, radio, and the Internet. Perhaps in a more so-called primitive era, integral spirituality could be relatively spontaneous, but in our day and age, we need to be intentional about it.

I am always of several minds as to where to begin—with spirit, soul, or body. All three are obviously essential. While studying theology I was taught that we should always respect the inherent hierarchy in the way we order things; hence one of my advisors counseled me to change the references in my thesis to "spirit, soul, and body," instead of "body, soul, and spirit," because the spirit (and the Spirit) is obviously the most important element.

On the other hand, Marco Vannini quotes Meister Eckhart as saying that, "The spirit cannot be perfect if the body and the soul are not perfect first; and therefore it is necessary to have full experience of body and soul, if one wants to have that of the spirit."[18] In the same vein, Benedetto Calati, one of the former priors general of my monastic congregation, the Camaldolese Benedictines, had a famous dictum regarding the foundation of monastic life and formation. "Before you can be a monk," he would often say, "you must be a Christian; and before being a Christian you must be a human being."

I think Don Benedetto was right. However, when I repeated his words to one of my friends who is a fine theologian, he did not agree, noting that in order to be fully human we *need* to be Christian, that Christianity and spirituality in general are what bring us to the fullness of our humanity. I think he was right, too! And apparently so does Vannini who, after quoting Meister Eckhart, says that "the contrary is also true: one does not even have true knowledge of soul and body without experience of the spirit."[19] Both views are important, and we must keep them in mind as we proceed.

Having said this, let me sum up my own position. We are not angels; we may never deny our humanity. As much as we may think of it as our burden, our humanity is our gift and our treasure. It is so precious that Jesus chose to take it on so that it could be raised up to the right hand of the Father in glory. At the same time, the spiritual dimension of being human cannot be denied. If we deny our spiritual dimension, we are in some way not fully human! So what I will argue from the very start is that our spirituality is not something we add onto ourselves, not something we cover ourselves with, not even something "supernatural": it is the very center and source of our being. It is what holds us together, body and soul.

Questions of Method

As I noted in the preface, each chapter of this book includes practical considerations regarding questions of method. Let us conclude this first chapter with an overview of the actual process of meditation, laying out some techniques that can help lead us to greater interiority. Here is a summary from the famous Indian Swami Muktananda that I have used for many years:

> There are four factors involved in meditation: *the object of medita-*
> *tion,* which is the inner self; *mantra,* which is the vibration of the
> self; *asana,* the posture in which we can sit comfortably for a long
> time; and natural *pranayama* [control of the breath], which arises
> when we repeat the mantra with love and reverence. These four
> factors are interrelated, and when they come together, meditation
> occurs in a very natural manner.[20]

I tend to re-order these a bit: object, posture, breath, and mantra.

We will obviously spend a good deal of time discussing the object of our meditation, and in a sense each of the chapters in this book directly addresses a specific aspect of the object of meditation.

With regard to the actual practice of meditation, let us start out very simply. If you already have a practice that works for you, please feel free to stay with it. As the ancient monks used to say, "A tree that gets uprooted too often doesn't grow deep roots." If, however, you are new to the practice of meditation, I suggest the following:

• Sit as upright as possible, letting the vertebrae of your spine rest comfortably one on top of the other. Let your shoulders drop and raise the crown of the head directly up toward the ceiling. If you are sitting on the floor, make yourself a solid foundation, with your knees and buttocks on the floor (or the latter on a cushion), offering the rest of your body as much support as possible. The various *asanas* (body positions) assumed in yogic exercises of *hatha* yoga are invaluable here: lotus, half-lotus, or the perfect pose. If you are sitting in a chair, plant both feet firmly but gently on the ground. Whether you are sitting on the floor or in a chair, place your hands gently in your lap or on your legs in a way that will remain comfortable for you during the entire time of sitting. Lower your eyelids gently until they are in a position that is neither open nor closed, as if sleeping—but do not sleep!

• Breathe gently, normally, quietly, through your nose, paying close attention to each breath to make you aware of your own body and the life force that runs through you. Perhaps it will be necessary for you to begin by taking several deep breaths to fill you up and calm your body down, but from then on, your lungs can function quite well without your permission. Your job is simply to be aware.

• Like Muktananda and many Hindus and some Buddhists, I too—and many Christians I know—have found great benefit in prayer from the use of a word, what is referred to by the Sanskrit term *mantra*. We will deal more with mantra in the next chapter. But for now, instead of using a mantra, I would like to recommend an exercise that I often find helpful to center myself, to focus on praying "the way in." It is the Zen exercise of merely counting our breaths, from one to ten, being aware, being aware, being aware of every breath. This exercise is not only a good beginning; for some Zen practitioners it is a practice that suffices for many years. Here is how Philip Kapleau records Yasutani Roshi's teaching in *The Three Pillars of Zen*:

    • When you have established a correct posture, take a deep breath, hold it momentarily, then exhale slowly and quietly. Repeat this two or three times, always breathing through the nose. After that, breathe naturally. When you have accustomed yourself to this routine, one deep breath at the beginning will suffice. After that, breathe naturally, without trying to manipulate your breath . . .

    • The easiest [method for concentration] for beginners is counting incoming and outgoing breaths. The value of this particular exercise lies in the fact that all the reasoning is excluded and the discriminative mind put at rest. Thus the waves of thought are stilled and a gradual one-pointedness of mind achieved. To start with, count both inhalations and exhalations. When you inhale, concentrate on "one"; when you exhale, on "two"; and so on up to "ten." Then you return to "one" and once more count up to "ten," continuing as before.[21]

Should you go on to "eleven" or "twelve" or "twenty-three," then this is a sign that you have lost awareness, so gently return to "one" and start all over again. If you prefer, or perhaps later, you may adapt this exercise in the way the late Jesuit priest and Zen master Enomiya-Lassalle taught: if you are distracted, just count the inhalations, and if you need to counteract drowsiness, just count the exhalations.[22]

Ultimately, of course, we concentrate on the breath only long enough to slow ourselves down and make ourselves aware of the fact that we are breathing. From then on, we need to let the word, or mantra, set the pace and frequency of the breath.

If you are worried that this is not enough prayer for you in some way, don't worry! The real prayer is your intention of quieting yourself and being available. Real prayer is being present to the Spirit who is already present to us, though we are usually unaware; your prayer will be longing for conscious contact with the Lord of Love.

2

JESUS ON PRAYER

The Spirit, who can be realized by the pure in heart,
who is life, light, truth, space . . .
who is beyond words,
who is joy abiding—
this is the Spirit dwelling in my heart.

—Chandogya Upanishad, III.XIV.2

Whenever you pray, go into your room and shut the door and pray to
your Father who is in secret; and your Father who sees in secret will
reward you.

—Matthew 6:6

It would be absurd to talk about Christian prayer and Christian meditation without talking about how Jesus prayed and Jesus' teachings on prayer. We don't often think of Jesus as a "meditator"; there are no clear mentions of Jesus meditating in the sense that we normally speak or think of meditation. A number of apocryphal legends tell of Jesus spending some of the "lost years" (when he was between the ages of twelve and thirty, a time that is unaccounted for in the Gospels) in India studying with yogis, but we have no historical proof of that.

Bede Griffiths describes Jesus as having reached in his prayer what the Hindus call the state of *sahaja samadhi*, the highest state beyond the active and the contemplative life, a state in which one "can be a contemplative, in perfect stillness, and at the same time fully active."

> Many Christians interpret Jesus in the New Testament simply as a
> man going about doing good, helping people and always busy and
> active, and they do not realize that he had gone beyond. In his six

19

weeks in the desert and in the depths of his being he was enjoying pure *samadhi*. He was a pure contemplative, always abiding with the Father as the source of his being, and always seeing what the Father does as the source of his action. He is in that state of transcendent awareness in which he is one with the Father, and at the same time perfectly natural and human.[1]

We don't know exactly how Jesus prayed; we don't know exactly what he did, or if he followed a set pattern or formula. We do know that he went off by himself, as in the desert during the forty days before he began his public ministry, and that he quite often escaped to lonely and deserted places to pray. Luke, for example, tells us that "during those days he went out to the mountain to pray; and he spent the night in prayer to God" (Luke 6:12).[2] So we do know that there was something hidden and quiet about the way that Jesus prayed. Perhaps that's why when he taught his disciples something about prayer, he said,

> And whenever you pray, do not be like the hypocrites; for they love to stand and pray in the synagogues and at the street corners, so that they may be seen by others. Truly I tell you, they have received their reward. But whenever you pray, go into your room and shut the door and pray to your Father who is in secret; and your Father who sees in secret will reward you. (Matt 6:5-6)

Eastern Christian writers love this passage, and they interpret the phrase "go into your room" or "go into your inner closet" as meaning "go into the chamber of your heart." Here is how St. Dimitri of Rostov interprets it:

> The closet is twofold, outer and inner, material and spiritual;
> the material place is of wood and stone,
> the spiritual closet is the heart or mind . . .
> the inner spiritual closet . . . holds God and all the Kingdom of
>   heaven . . .[3]

So, if the Eastern teachers are correct, we have here a first hint about the interior way of prayer from Jesus himself: when you pray, do not stand and pray in the synagogues and at the street corners; when you pray, go into your heart.

A second hint can be found in his mention of the Father "who
sees in secret." To understand Jesus' prayer, and to understand how
we can enter into and share in the prayer of Jesus, we must understand one very simple truth: Jesus had a unique and extraordinary
relationship with God; if there is nothing else that Christians claim
about Jesus, it is this. St. Paul describes the relationship twice in
the Letter to the Colossians: "For in him all the fullness of God
was pleased to dwell" (Col 1:19); and "For in him the whole fullness of deity dwells bodily" (Col 2:9). These are clearly descriptions
of Jesus' own personal divinity. What we must keep in mind, however, is that there is an important relational aspect to Jesus' divinity: Jesus was so intimate with God as to call God *Abba*, a much
more tender word than our English translation, "Father." And, as
part of that relational aspect, Jesus wants other human beings to
share in the relationship with God that he himself has.

Paul follows up his description of the "fullness of deity" dwelling
in Jesus bodily by saying ". . . and you have come to fullness in
him" (Col 2:10), just as John writes in the prologue to his Gospel,
"From his fullness we have all received, grace upon grace" (John
1:16). In Jesus' Farewell Discourse, he prays "that they may all be
one. As you, Father, are in me and I am in you, may they also be in
us" (John 17:21). And, in a powerful and vivid image, Jesus brings
together the two dimensions of the relational aspect of his divinity:
"I am the vine, you are the branches" (John 15:5). How much closer
can we get than that? To Jesus and to the Father! The same sap
running through Jesus runs through us, and that sap is, of course,
the Holy Spirit, who is none other than Jesus' love relationship
with God, his *Abba*, and with us. The sap is the Spirit.

It is somehow not enough to simply worship Jesus, though that
is an excellent and necessary place to start. We receive from his
fullness. We are, as the prayer during the preparation of the gifts
at the Mass in the Roman Rite says, meant to "share in the divinity
of Christ who humbled himself to share in our humanity."

The Our Father

When Jesus' disciples asked him directly, "Lord, teach us to pray," he responded by giving them the words of what is commonly known as the "Lord's Prayer," the Our Father. We have two versions of this prayer, one in the Gospel of Matthew and the other in the Gospel of Luke. Here is Matthew's version:

> Pray then in this way:
> Our Father in heaven,
> hallowed be your name.
> Your kingdom come.
> Your will be done,
> on earth as it is in heaven.
> Give us this day our daily bread.
> And forgive us our debts,
> as we also have forgiven our debtors.
> And do not bring us to the time of trial,
> but rescue us from the evil one. (Matt 6:9-13)

The wording of Luke's version is slightly different, but both versions are set in a context that makes some mention of secret, hidden prayer. In Matthew's Gospel, the text of the Lord's Prayer follows on the scripture verses discussed above, the saying with regard to going into your room and shutting the door and praying to your Father who is in secret (Matt 6:6). Luke, on the other hand, sets the scene a little differently. He simply says that the disciples ask Jesus to teach them to pray after he has been "praying in a certain place." I imagine that Jesus has been alone in one of his hidden places again, with the Father who sees in secret, and that Jesus' teaching on prayer is coming out of that experience.

In Matthew's Gospel, the Lord's Prayer is followed immediately by words on the forgiveness of sins, as if that were the most important point. Jesus says, "For if you forgive others their trespasses, your heavenly Father will also forgive you; but if you do not forgive others, neither will your Father forgive your trespasses" (Matt 6:14-15).[4]

In Luke's Gospel, the teaching on the Our Father is followed by words about persistence in prayer. Jesus makes the comparison of going at midnight to a friend and asking to borrow three loaves of bread to feed some unexpected guests. Even though the friend may not give anything out of friendship, at least he will get up and give whatever is needed because of the other's persistence. The message here seems to be that persistence is the most important point of the teaching on prayer.

Shortly after the teaching on the Our Father, Matthew gives us his own version of the exhortation to persistence. Jesus says, "Ask, and it will be given you; search, and you will find; knock, and the door will be opened for you" (Matt 7:7). Search, and you will find—where? In your own heart! Knock—where? At the door to the chamber of your own heart! Ask, and it will be given—poured into your very heart. What shall you find there in your heart? God's will! The prophet Jeremiah tells us: "The days are surely coming . . . when I will make a new covenant: I will put my law within them, and I will write it on their hearts," (Jer 31:31, 33). And St. Paul writes: "The word is near you, on your lips and in your heart" (Rom 10:8).

In Matthew's Gospel, Jesus continues by saying,

> For everyone who asks receives, and everyone who searches finds, and for everyone who knocks, the door will be opened. Is there anyone among you who, if your child asks for bread, will give a stone? Or if the child asks for a fish, will give a snake? If you then, who are evil, know how to give good gifts to your children, how much more will your Father in heaven give good things to those who ask him! (Matt 7:8-11)

Luke's version of this saying is more specific. He says: "How much more will the heavenly Father give the *Holy Spirit* to those who ask him!" (Luke 11:13). What we are really praying for is that the gift of the Holy Spirit be poured into our hearts or, perhaps more accurately, that we may be aware of and in communion with the gift we have already received.

The Spirit: God's Love Poured Out into Our Hearts

Most of our prayer as children is a matter of asking for things. And quite often most of our prayer as adults is the same. We reach the end of our rope and suddenly turn to prayer, maybe even looking to bargain with God, as if we could change God's mind. I do not mean to suggest that this is wrong—after all, at least it involves some recognition that there is a power greater than ourselves. Neither do I mean to imply that miracles don't happen. It is just that it is important to realize that prayer does not change God; prayer changes us! Prayer doesn't change God's heart because God is and always was and always will be total love. Prayer changes our hearts to receive what is in some way already there, already poured into us, always available—the Holy Spirit. How often does Jesus say in the Gospel to people he has healed, "Go now, *your faith* has saved you"?[5]

For me, the center of the Gospel message can be found in the Gospel of John, when Jesus cries out:

> Let anyone who is thirsty come to me, and let the one who believes in me drink. As the scripture has said, "Out of the believer's heart shall flow rivers of living water." (John 7:37-38)

After quoting these words, John adds somewhat parenthetically that Jesus "said this about the Spirit, which believers in him were to receive" (John 7:39).

What does this simple passage from the Gospel of John mean? Let us turn to St. Paul for help in interpreting it. His letters are replete with references to the same theme, but it is perhaps most succinctly stated in Romans 5:5: "God's love has been poured into our hearts through the Holy Spirit that has been given to us."[6] The love of God has been poured directly into our hearts, the deepest part of our being. Put the two scripture passages together and the whole picture becomes clear: the love of God, which is the Spirit that Jesus promises in the Gospels, has been poured directly into us, into our deepest center, into our heart of hearts (what we will refer to later as our spirit), and that same Spirit is meant then to flow out from our hearts.

The Holy Spirit is referred to by many different images, often as wind, sometimes as fire, but in this passage from the Gospel of John as a life-giving stream, a stream that will flow out from our very hearts. The psalms present this marvelous image:

> There is a river whose streams make glad the city of God,
>   the holy habitation of the Most High. (Ps 46:4)

That "city of God," the holy habitation of the Most High, can be understood to be our own body. As the *Chandogya Upanishad* says, "In the city of Brahman is a secret dwelling place, the lotus of the heart."[7] And, from the lotus of our heart, a stream flows through the city to make it glad, and John tells us that that stream is none other than the Holy Spirit. The Spirit that is in us is not meant to stay put—it is power. Especially in Luke's Gospel, the Spirit is usually associated with *dynamis*, "power," that is meant to flow through us, course through our veins, and pour out of us in love and service. Prayer, the way of contemplative prayer and meditation, is our means of accessing that power, that Spirit that has been poured into us, accessing it as Jesus did when he went out to the deserted places.

We have been taught how to pray "out," to God "out there." It seems that even Jesus taught us to do this when he said that we are to pray to "Our Father in heaven." We are taught to call out to the heavens, to Mary and to the saints, and to offer praise and thanks—and all those things are right and just, and some people may spend an entire life praying in only that outward way. But there is another way, too, and it is a way that is open to everyone. The problem is that everyone may not be aware of it.

Perhaps the reason for this problem is that we have been defining "heaven" in too limited a manner, as in the hymn that refers to "some heaven light years away." What if heaven is also to be found in our own hearts? Consider the words of Isaac of Syria, a seventh-century saint:

> Try to enter your inner treasure house
> and you will see the treasure house of heaven.
> For both the one and the other are the same,
> and the one and the same entrance reveals them both.
> The ladder leading to the kingdom is within you, that is, in
>   your soul.[8]

When people become aware of this reality—that the kingdom of heaven is inside them—then praying "the way in," taking ownership of that reality, becomes a necessity, as it was for the one who found the treasure hidden in the field, or the one who found the pearl of great price and sold everything to buy it.[9]

Finding the Treasure

There are two parables from Matthew that speak of the interior way of realizing God's presence.

> "The kingdom of heaven is like a mustard seed that someone took and sowed in his field; it is the smallest of all the seeds, but when it has grown it is the greatest of shrubs and becomes a tree, so that the birds of the air come and make nests in its branches."
>
> He told them another parable: "The kingdom of heaven is like yeast that a woman took and mixed in with three measures of flour until all of it was leavened." (Matt 13:31-33)

Both of these parables point clearly to the way within. The seed that becomes a mighty shrub—a tiny little thing that contains, in potential, something huge—is such a powerful symbol of organic growth, of interiority unfolding into life. Equally powerful is the image of the yeast saturating the dough and bringing it to fullness and fruition. Listen to these words of the seventeenth-century French mystic Jean-Pierre de Caussade:

> This is what being holy means. It is the mustard seed, which is almost too small to be recognized or harvested, the drachma of the Gospels, the treasure that no one finds, as it is thought to be too well hidden to be looked for. But what is the secret of finding this treasure? There isn't one! It is offered to us all the time and wherever we are. All creatures, friends or foes, pour it out in abundance, and it flows through every fiber of our body and soul until it reaches the very core of our being . . . God's activity runs through the universe. It wells up and around and penetrates every created being. Where they are, it is also.[10]

When de Caussade says that there is no secret to finding this treasure, I am reminded of the image used often in India of the musk in the deer, referring to the indwelling Divine. Human beings are like the deer that smell the musk and go in search of it among the grasses, not knowing all the while that it is emanating from themselves. Where is this seed? In us! Where is the yeast? Inside us—permeating and penetrating and flowing through us. What is this yeast, this seed? It is none other than the *dynamis*-power of the Holy Spirit.

Let us conclude our reflections by returning to the *Chandogya Upanishad* with which we began this chapter:

> The Spirit, who can be realized by the pure in heart,
> who is life, light, truth, space,
> who gives rise to all works, all desires, all odors, all tastes,
> who is beyond words,
> who is joy abiding—
> this is the Spirit dwelling in my heart.
> Smaller than a grain of rice,
> smaller than a grain of barley,
> smaller than a mustard seed,
> smaller than a grain of millet is the Spirit.
> This is the Spirit dwelling in my heart,
> greater than the earth,
> greater than the sky,
> greater than all the worlds.[11]

Questions of Method

In chapter 1, we introduced Swami Muktananda's four aspects of meditation: object, posture, breathing, and mantra. Here and throughout the rest of this book as we discuss "questions of method" we will continue using these as our framework, revisiting one or more of them to consider them in greater depth.

Clearly, this entire chapter has addressed the "object" of meditation. We have looked at what we could glean of Jesus' own prayer and, with that as a basis, we have concerned ourselves with the prayer that Jesus taught us, the Lord's Prayer, and what it has to say about the kingdom within us, the treasure who is none other than the Holy Spirit, the stream of life-giving water inside of us that reveals and connects us to God.

With regard to posture, we spoke in chapter 1 of the necessity for an erect position, one that is comfortable and yet alert. A yoga teacher once said that this upright posture is the sign of our dignity as human beings, that we are the only animal that can carry itself in this way. An ancient Christian writer, Diodore of Tarsus, expressed the same view in the fourth century when he said that our upright posture indicates that we are the leaders in the created order whose mission is to prolong the work of God.[12] The erectness of our posture is the sign of an even greater dignity—our union with Christ, for, as we saw earlier in this chapter, we are meant to share in the fullness of Christ. To use the words of St. Paul, we are to "put on the Lord Jesus Christ" (Rom 13:14), to have within us "the same mind . . . that was in Christ Jesus" (Phil 2:5)—and our bearing reflects this.

Concerning the word that we use as a mantra, let us consider what Jesus said to his disciples before teaching them the Lord's Prayer, the verses that in Matthew's Gospel actually serve as an introduction to the Lord's Prayer:

> When you are praying, do not heap up empty phrases as the Gentiles do; for they think that they will be heard because of their many words. Do not be like them, for your Father knows what you need before you ask him. (Matt 6:7-8)

Do not heap up empty phrases! Get to the point! An old monk taught me when I entered the monastery that he always tried to reduce every prayer to its simplest element, and so the Hail Mary became for him, "Mary, pray for us!" Do not heap up empty phrases! The author of *The Cloud of Unknowing*, a fourteenth-century mystic widely thought to have been a Carthusian monk, notes that contemplatives rarely pray in words, but if they do, their words are few—"The fewer the better," he says, "and a word of one syllable is more suited to the spiritual nature of this work than longer ones."[13]

He then gives the example of someone struck suddenly by a disaster; that person would yell out "Help!" or "Fire!" and not waste a lot of time being eloquent or loquacious. So, he says, in a similar way,

> . . . we can understand the efficacy of one little interior word, not merely spoken or thought but surging up from the depth of [our] spirit, the expression of [our] whole being . . . This simple prayer bursting from the depths of your own spirit touches the heart of Almighty God more certainly than some long psalm mumbled mindlessly under your breath.[14]

It is worth noting that the word, according to the author of the *Cloud*, should not be something imposed from a source outside of or above us, but rather something that surges up or bursts out from the depths of our own spirit.

It could be said that the Lord's Prayer, which according to Jesus is a synopsis of all prayer, can be simplified even further. Jesus himself gives us a shorter version, one that he used in his own prayer, one that surged up from the depths of his own spirit in the Garden of Gethsemane: "Your will be done" (Matt 26:39, Mark 14:36, Luke 22:42). In sorrow and in pain, in sickness and in health, "Your will be done." What a mantra that is!

So, I urge you to find for yourself a word or a short phrase, if you do not already have one, a word or a phrase that surges up from the depths of your being. Perhaps you want to unite yourself with Jesus in making his words—"Your will be done"—your own mantra. Whatever you choose, attach it to your breath and let it carry you to the depths of your being where the Spirit, like a stream of life-giving water, is to be found.

3

ST. PAUL ON PRAYER

As long as I am seated in this meditation . . .
I renounce, for the duration of this meditation,
my body, all food and all passions . . .
Thus have I attained to equanimity and to my own self-nature.

—From the Jain Nityanaimittika-pathavali

Likewise the Spirit helps us in our weakness; for we do not know how
to pray as we ought, but that very Spirit intercedes with sighs too deep
for words.

—Romans 8:26

In this chapter we will begin by looking at two themes that shape St. Paul's view of prayer. The first is his understanding of the nature of the human person and the second is his insight into the nature of prayer as ultimately the prayer of the Spirit, the prayer of Jesus. With this as a foundation, we will then move on to reflect on the implications of St. Paul's view of prayer, especially as they relate to levels of prayer, the inward journey, and what has been referred to as the "way of paradox."

St. Paul's Understanding of the Nature of the Human Person

In chapter 1 we discussed the anthropological view of the human person as not simply body and soul, but as body, soul, and spirit. This is a view that Paul held, and its clearest articulation can be found in his First Letter to the Thessalonians:

> May the God of peace himself sanctify you entirely; and may your spirit and soul and body be kept sound and blameless at the coming of our Lord Jesus Christ. (1 Thess 5:23)

As body (in Greek, *soma*), the human is part of the whole physical universe, having evolved out of the physical universe, from matter and life. As soul (*psyche*), the human is the head of the universe—matter having come into consciousness in the form of an individual. But then, like matter itself, the soul has the potential to open to the *pneuma*, the spirit, which is the point at which the human opens to the Spirit of God.[1]

The body-soul dualism with which we are familiar comes from Greek, specifically Platonic, philosophy. Jacques Dupuis sees such dualism as the source of the "pessimism of Greek philosophy regarding the body." According to the Greeks, he says,

> life is destined to death; since the body (*soma*) is a tomb (*sema*), salvation can only consist in being freed of it through evasion. One thinks of the contrast between the Greek belief in the immortality of the soul and the Christian faith in the resurrection of bodies . . .[2]

When we look at the Judeo-Christian biblical view of the human person, we find something quite different from the Greek view. In order to understand biblical anthropology, how the scriptures see the makeup of the human person, we have to set aside for a moment our old conceptions of body and soul as two antagonistic entities, or the idea that the body is a "tomb" or a "prison" for the soul. From the biblical point of view, body and soul are always a "substantial unity," even though they may be a unity that can be approached from different angles—from the viewpoint of corporeality or from the viewpoint of psychology.

To the Hebrew mind—and to the mind of Paul and other New Testament writers—there is no such thing as a body without a soul, or a soul without a body. In the Bible, the term "flesh" (*basar, sarx*) means the entire complex, the living flesh. The human being leaves the hands of God as a "living soul," an embodied soul, an en-souled body that is essentially one. The second story of creation in Genesis makes this quite clear: God breathes into the clay and it becomes a *nephesh*-soul. We do not simply "have" a soul: we *are* a soul, *psyche* or *nephesh*. If the soul disappears, what is left is not a body, but dust of the earth, "dust returning to dust."[3] Hebrew doesn't even have a word for a dead body. It is no longer a body if it is dead; it is merely dust. The living human person, on the other hand, is an incarnated spirit who participates in being to such an extent that St. Peter defines the goal of life in this way: that we "may become partakers of the divine nature" (2 Pet 1:4).[4]

So, from this perspective, the body cannot be "at war" with the soul. If anything, what biblical anthropology does is add a new element that is only hinted at in Greek philosophy—*ruah, pneuma,* spirit.[5] This is not to say that the notion of conflict is eliminated; rather, the Bible describes the conflict from an entirely different perspective. Certainly it can be said that God's plans and desires appear to be in conflict with the creature's desires and that holiness conflicts with sin. We can also find biblical references to the flesh being a burden that weighs down the spirit. For example, in Galatians 5:17 Paul writes, "What the flesh desires is opposed to the Spirit, and what the Spirit desires is opposed to the flesh . . ." Even here, however, the contrast is not between the body and the soul, but between the body-soul complex and the spirit.

One example of Paul's use of the term "spirit" in this sense can be found in the First Letter to the Corinthians:

> Those who are unspiritual (*psykikos*) do not receive the gifts of God's Spirit, for they are foolishness to them, and they are unable to understand them because they are discerned spiritually. Those who are spiritual (*pneumatikos*) discern all things, and they are themselves subject to no one else's scrutiny. (1 Cor 2:14-15)

Paul later says:

> And so, brothers and sisters, I could not speak to you as spiritual (*pneumatikos*) people, but rather as people of the flesh (*sarkikos*), as infants in Christ. (1 Cor 3:1)

Clearly, then, it is just as inadequate to be merely "of the soul" (*anthropos psykikos*) as it is to be "of the flesh" (*anthropos sarkikos*). There is something beyond both—to be "of the spirit," *anthropos pneumatikos,* because the spirit brings both the body and the soul to fruition. Tomas Spidlik explains that the philosophical *dichotomy* (body-soul) had to be completed by the theological *trichotomy* (body-soul-spirit), which was to become traditional in Eastern Christian thought.[6]

The Prayer of the Spirit, the Prayer of Jesus

What is the nature and function of our spirit? The answer to this question forms the second theme that shapes St. Paul's view of prayer, and it is absolutely crucial to our prayer life. We find Paul's answer spelled out in his Letter to the Romans:

> . . . all who are led by the Spirit of God are children of God. For you did not receive a spirit of slavery to fall back into fear, but you have received a spirit of adoption. When we cry, "Abba! Father!" it is that very Spirit bearing witness with our spirit that we are children of God, and if children, then heirs, heirs of God and joint heirs with Christ . . . (Rom 8:14-17)

The Holy Spirit bearing witness with the human spirit! Further, Paul says,

> Likewise the Spirit helps us in our weakness; for we do not know how to pray as we ought, but that very Spirit intercedes with sighs too deep for words. And God, who searches the heart, knows what is the mind of the Spirit, because the Spirit intercedes for the saints according to the will of God. (Rom 8:26-27)

The astounding thing is that what we think of as "our" prayer is in some way not even our prayer; it is the prayer of the Holy Spirit who has been poured into our hearts. What we are actually attempting to do through our meditation is to come into conscious contact with the prayer of the Holy Spirit, Jesus' own prayer that the Spirit is humming in our hearts. To use a different image, recall the saying of Jesus about the stream of living water that is to flow out of the believer's own heart (John 7:38) and consider these words from the book that ends the New Testament, the Book of Revelation:

> The Spirit and the bride say, "Come."
> And let everyone who hears say, "Come."
> And let everyone who is thirsty come.
> Let anyone who wishes take the water of life as a gift. (Rev 22:17)

So our role is not a passive one. We are the Bride and we sing the
Spirit's song; we sing with the Spirit who is in us praying in sighs too
deep for words, except for one word perhaps, the same word that
Jesus had ever on his lips and in his heart and what St. Paul tells us
the Spirit is always praying inside of our own hearts: *Abba!*

Levels of Prayer

All the different forms of prayer, all the various ways in which we
pray, as Howard Bleichner writes, flow from the reality that we
are creatures of many levels of consciousness. We might, for example, pray the rosary out loud or to ourselves, saying the words
of the prayers while on another level of our mind—beneath the
words—we're also thinking about the mysteries, events in Jesus'
life.

At other times we might talk to God or to Jesus as if conversing
with a close friend. When I think of this kind of prayer I am reminded of Tevye in *Fiddler on the Roof.* A Jewish writer once described him as having as much a horizontal relationship with God
as a vertical one. Tevye doesn't look up to heaven to talk to God;
rather, Tevye turns his head kind of at an angle, like an old friend:
"On the one hand . . . on the other hand . . ." consulting God
about his plans and his troubles.

At still other times we "may fall silent . . . as [we] might with a
good friend with whom for the moment all words have been ex-
hausted and [we] are content to sit quietly together."[7] The story is
told of an old monk who used to sit day after day in the back of the
church—no beads, no book, never even seeming to move his lips.
One day someone asked him, "What do you do all day, just sitting
there?" And the old man answered, "I look at him; he looks at me."

Occasionally there can be prayer that is wordless adoration, an
upsweep of bliss that comes from realizing that we are in the
presence of God, when we are suddenly made aware of the fact
that we are surrounded by the Divine on every side. To borrow
the words of the psalmist:

> O LORD, you have searched me and known me.
> You know when I sit down and when I rise up;

> you discern my thoughts from far away.
> You search out my path and my lying down,
>   and are acquainted with all my ways.
> Even before a word is on my tongue,
>   O LORD, you know it completely.
> You hem me in, behind and before,
>   and lay your hand upon me. (Ps 139:1-5)

It has been said that God is closer to us than we are to ourselves. Or, as the Qur'an teaches:

> Verily, We created human beings and know what their soul
>   whispers,
> for We are closer to them than their jugular vein.[8]

Perhaps a deeper level yet is when we realize that God is in us, that we are temples of the Holy Spirit ourselves, that the love of God has been poured into our hearts, that the stream of living water is flowing within us. As St. Augustine in his *Confessions* says,

> You were within me, and I was outside, and it was there I searched
> for you . . . On entering into myself I saw, as it were with the eye
> of my soul, what was beyond the eye of the soul, beyond my spirit:
> your immutable light.[9]

Beyond my soul, beyond my spirit! Ultimately, at the deepest level of our being, it is God's Spirit who "not only *teaches* us to pray but *prays in us* . . . returning to God the worship of the Son in the Spirit."[10]

At the centenary event celebrating the life of Bede Griffiths, a priest who had had Fr. Bede as a spiritual director told us of a sharp admonition Fr. Bede had given him regarding prayer, an admonition based on this teaching of St. Paul. "You have fabricated an idol who is an object!" Fr. Bede had told the priest. "God is not an object, and you are not the subject. The subject of prayer is God, who prays in Jesus in the Spirit." Fr. Bede had gone on to explain that the point of prayer is not so much to make an effort to contact God. "Instead," Fr. Bede had said, "you must strive to remove everything that prevents you from listening to God speaking in you."

From the Jain tradition, we have words that describe the attitude described by Fr. Bede:

> As long as I am seated in this meditation,
> I shall patiently suffer all calamities that may befall me,
> be they caused by an animal, a human being, or a god.
> I renounce, for the duration of this meditation,
> my body, all food and all passions.
> Attachment, aversion, fear, sorrow, joy, anxiety, self-pity . . .
> all these I abandon with body, mind and speech.
> Thus have I attained to equanimity and to my own self-nature.
> May this state of equanimity be with me until I attain to
>   salvation.[11]

So here we understand that prayer is listening, and preparation
for prayer means removing all that distracts us from hearing God
speaking in us.

Through the Self

Our discussion has centered on praying the interior way, taking the
inward journey, but it is important to emphasize that the journey is
not a matter of simple navel-gazing. This is a critical point, especially
in an age when we are so fixated on "I, me, mine." As John Main
taught, the inner journey can tap into the self-preoccupation that
often masquerades as spirituality. There is a danger that the interior
journey can lead us to a kind of solipsism, a place where we get
ensnared in the trap of our own subjective experience instead of
being "relieved of the bondage of self," to use the language of Twelve
Step programs. We must remember that what we are seeking through
this ascent to the depths of the heart is the temple within, the place
where the Holy Spirit dwells. We are going through ourselves to get
beyond ourselves. The journey is through our own experience,
through our own souls, through our griefs, joys, and pains—but it is
decidedly *through* them, in the belief that there is something on the
other side of them if we don't get caught up in them, in the belief
that our deepest selves lie hidden, as St. Paul says, "with Christ in
God" (Col 3:3). In the words of Anthony Bloom:

So it is inward we must turn . . . but inward in a very special way
. . . It is not a journey into my own inwardness, it is a journey *through*
my own self, in order to emerge from the deepest level of self into
the place where [God] is, the point at which God and I meet.[12]

If the anthropology that I have proposed of body, soul, and spirit
is to be trusted, then "the place where God is, the point at which
God and I meet" of which Archbishop Bloom speaks is our spirit—
beyond our body, beyond our soul. Fr. John Main too teaches that
"the essence of meditation is taking the attention off ourselves and
looking forward, beyond ourselves into the mystery of God; of
traveling beyond ourselves" into God's love, into union.[13]

In the silence and stillness of meditation, he says,

we open our hearts to the eternal silence of God, to be swept out
of ourselves, beyond ourselves by the power of that silence.[14]

The Way of Paradox

In his excellent book on Meister Eckhart, *The Way of Paradox*,
Dom Cyprian Smith speaks of two different approaches to the
interior journey. The first path is that of much of modern psycho-
analysis, the penetration to the deeper levels of the mind, the slow,
gradual filtering through the contents of the unconscious mind.
As the unconscious reveals itself through dreams and symbols, we
pay close attention, dismissing nothing, ignoring nothing. Everything is pondered, welcomed, accepted, and gradually worked
through, with care taken not to get trapped or overwhelmed at
any level. "If we patiently and persistently follow this serpentine
path into the depths of ourselves," Dom Cyprian promises

. . . we shall discover, at the cost of some danger [!], unsuspected
sources of energy for good or for ill—buried treasures, guarded by
dragons and gnomes and if we follow the path right to the end,
beyond the merely psychological, we shall finally come to the deepest level of all, the "treasure hidden in the field" of which the gospel
speaks—the pure undifferentiated consciousness, stripped of all
that is egoistical and personal, the central core of our nature, where
the light of God shines.[15]

This path is not exclusive to psychiatry; it is what is taught and practiced in certain schools of Buddhism and Hindu meditation, and by many Christian mystics of the visionary and imaginative type—Julian of Norwich and Henry Suso, for example—for whom the revelation of God rises up from deep levels of consciousness, coming through visions and symbols that are meditated on until their meaning is grasped.

But there is another path, which Dom Cyprian says is the path taken by practitioners of, for example, the Zen school of Buddhism, and it has its counterpart in the mysticism of Evagrius of Pontus, *The Cloud of Unknowing*, John of the Cross, and Meister Eckhart— and this is the path known as the *via negativa*.

> It aims straight for the goal, the deepest layer of the mind, the pure essence of consciousness, which is the Image of God in us. If, as we penetrate further toward the centre, images and symbols arise, promises of new desires and new possibilities, they are to be ignored and passed by, until the Central Core is reached, where we can become rooted and grounded in God.[16]

It is not easy to ignore and pass by the sometimes beautiful and attractive things that seem to arise from our spiritual depths, but there is a promise of something more if we do. At first it might seem that the promise is that of arriving at this "Central Core" but, according to Dom Cyprian, the promise of something more exists even there:

> Then, strengthened and enlightened by that, we can ascend slowly to the light, unlocking caverns and treasures on our way, if that seems right . . . The first prerequisite is to find God in the deepest core of ourselves, and this is done by detachment, by letting go of all in us that is not God, until the spark of awareness awakens in us, which Eckhart calls "the Birth of God in the Soul." There is nothing final or definitive about it; it is only a start. There remains the ascent, the gradual exploring of all that was previously neglected. As this process goes on, the spark of consciousness steadily grows until it gradually illuminates the whole mind. It is the work of a lifetime.[17]

The experience of undifferentiated consciousness, then, should it be granted us, is still only a start! From that prime experience comes greater knowledge of self and also greater love for the world. In the Christian tradition, this is the "incarnational" element, the stream of living water flowing back from out of the believer's heart.

Questions of Method

One of the best practical tools that we can use on our inward journey is the mantra. An image I like to use for this term is that of a pebble dropped into a pool of water. We attach our breath to this mantra and use it to sink to the depths of our consciousness. Let us now look a bit more closely at what exactly a mantra is.

The Sanskrit word *mantra* combines the root word *man* (to think) with the suffix *tra* (instrument or tool). Thus the word "mantra" means literally a "tool for thinking." A famous image used to describe the mantra is that of removing a thorn with a thorn. In other words, the mind needs something to do to keep it quiet and active at the same time, to turn its activity into a low manageable hum. So, we give it something to hold on to, a word, a simple prayer that sums up our intention, a mantra.

Dating back to the time of the creation of the ancient Hindu sacred texts, or Vedas, and since the earliest Buddhist period, the repetition of sacred phrases has been used as an aid for meditation— to purify and focus the mind, to offer devotion or thanks, or to protect and nurture spiritual activity. Some authors differentiate between three different kinds of mantras. Mantras of the first type, *bija* mantras or seed syllables, have no translatable meaning; they are pure sounds, such as OM.[18] There are also "mixed" mantras, which combine *bijas* with words that have translatable meaning. Finally, there are mantras known as *dharanis*, which are phrases that are similar in function to *bija* and "mixed" mantras but can be translated word for word, since each syllable has a specific meaning.

In the West some of these Hindu and Buddhist mantras have become well known, diffused especially by various recordings. Let us look at three examples.

In the Hindu tradition perhaps the most famous is the *gayatri* mantra, which is used to begin the three periods of prayer and meditation, known as *sandhyas*, that are normally observed by *rishis*, yogis, and observant Hindus at daybreak, midday, and night-fall. (As an interesting side note, the word *sandhya* also means "the silence between sounds." What a beautiful image for a time of meditation—the silence between sounds!) Our own Camaldolese monks at Shantivanam Ashram in India begin each of their prayer times with the *gayatri* mantra:

> OM *bhur bhuva svaha*
> *tat savitur varenyam*
> *bhargo devasya dhimahi*
> *dhiyo yo nah prachodyat*

This is how they translate it:

> OM! Salutations to the world beyond
> which is present in the earth, and in the heavens:
> let us meditate on the splendor of the giver of life.
> May that one illuminate our meditation.

The Buddhist tradition also has mantras. At the end of the Heart Sutra the Buddha introduces the *Prajnaparamita* mantra, the mantra of Transcendent Perfection. This mantra is recited in some form in many Zen centers and other places throughout the Mahayana Buddhist world. According to the Heart Sutra, "these syllabic sounds . . . contain the entire Perfection of Wisdom":

> This is the mantra that awakens every conscious stream into pure presence. This is the mantra of all mantras, the mantra that transmits the principles of incomparability and inconceivability, the mantra that instantly dissipates the apparent darkness of egocentric misery, the mantra that invokes only truth and does not acknowledge the separate self-existence of any falsehood:

> GATE GATE PARAGATE PARASAMGATE BODHI SVAHA

> Gone! Gone! Gone!
> Beyond even the beyond,
> into full enlightenment!
> So be it!

And then there is the beautiful Tibetan mantra, OM *mani padme hum*: the mantra of Avalokitesvara (Kwan Yin), the Bodhisattva of Compassion. This mantra is found inscribed everywhere in Tibet, in homes, on rocks and walls, and has become popular even in our own culture as a result of the spread of Tibetan Buddhist practice in the West. According to one story in the Tibetan tradition, Avalokitesvara, feeling compassion for the suffering of five hundred worms struggling for existence in a pit, took the form of a golden bee and, buzzing this mantra, flew over the pit. When the worms heard the sound of the six syllables they were completely freed from their suffering and reborn in a celestial realm. The most common translation of the mantra is "The jewel (*mani*) in the lotus (*padme*)"; the syllables OM and *hum* are untranslatable.[19] What the mantra has come to mean is this: the jewel symbolizes enlightened consciousness, and the lotus—a beautiful flower that has its roots in the mud—symbolizes ordinary consciousness. Thus, when consciousness has been trained, or perhaps (as the Upanishads would say) when the senses have been trained and the mind has been stilled, the jewel of enlightened consciousness is revealed in the heart of the lotus of everyday consciousness.[20]

A mantra, then, is in essence a short phrase or a word that has some power to it, some meaning behind it, and that does not require too much thought. It is already pregnant with meaning. Our use of a mantra is not at all like what we do when we meditate, as we say, "discursively," as on the mysteries of the rosary, or when we think about the details of Jesus' life. In using a mantra we don't apply analytic thinking; we don't get caught up in details. So, for example, some people use the sacred syllable OM, which has incredible resonance for them, signifying as it does the primal word, the Divine sound. I myself have used OM *mani padme hum*, because I find that the notion of "the jewel in the lotus" is weighted with meaning and serves as a simple, powerful image of that spark of the Divine hidden within the human heart.

What many mantras have in common is that they are expressed in a language that has a sacred resonance to it, as does Sanskrit. In the Roman Catholic tradition, our "sacred language" was for many centuries Latin. After the Second Vatican Council we for the most part did away with the use of Latin in favor of the vernacular, and although much was gained from this change, one of the complaints was that we also lost something very important. There is something to be said for the fact that the very sounds of a language can help to put us in touch with the sacred.

Another sacred language is Aramaic, since it was the language that Jesus himself used. In your own prayer, if you have a word or a phrase that you are already using as a mantra, please feel free to continue with it. Or, perhaps, if you would like to experiment with something new, you might try an Aramaic word, one in keeping with St. Paul's teaching on the prayer of the Spirit, what might be considered Jesus' own mantra—*Abba*.

4

CONTINUAL PRAYER—THE DESERT

For those who are practicing "stopping," they should retire to some quiet place, or better live in some quiet place, sitting erect and with earnest and zestful purpose seek to quiet and concentrate the mind . . . [which] should become like a mirror, reflecting things but not judging them nor retaining them.

—From the *Mahayana Buddhist* Shraddhotpada Shastra

Take up the whole armor of God, so that you may be able to withstand on that evil day, and having done everything, to stand firm . . . Pray in the Spirit at all times in every prayer and supplication. To that end keep alert and always persevere in supplication . . .

—Ephesians 6:13, 18

In chapter 3 we looked at two of the themes that shape St. Paul's view of prayer and considered some of the practical implications of those themes for our own prayer. Among the many other themes we could have chosen is one that is particularly fitting as an introduction to this chapter. That theme, which we are attributing here to St. Paul, derives of course from Jesus himself, and it is the exhortation to unceasing, continual prayer. Paul mentions often how he himself and others in the Christian community pray constantly, and he urges his readers to do the same. In his Letter to the Ephesians, for example, he urges them to "pray in the Spirit at all times in every prayer and supplication" (Eph 6:18); and in the First Letter to the Thessalonians he is unambiguous: "Rejoice always, pray without ceasing, give thanks in all circumstances; for this is the will of God in Christ Jesus for you" (1 Thess 5:16-18).

As with many other themes of St. Paul, I think we need to take this literally. If for the moment we can think of prayer as "conscious contact with God," then we can easily say about Jesus that he was always and in every circumstance in conscious contact with God—that he was literally praying "without ceasing." He knew the Father's will for him and was filled with the power of the Spirit.

How often we are shown the first Christians doing likewise. Commitment to prayer was one of the chief characteristics of the first Christians. In the Acts of the Apostles, for instance, we are told of how the believers gathered in prayer, whether at home, in the synagogue, or in the temple. In Acts 1:14 we read that they "were constantly devoting themselves to prayer"; in Acts 2:42 we learn that they "devoted themselves to the apostles' teaching and fellowship, to the breaking of bread and the prayers."

This desire to pray constantly would eventually develop into what would come to be known as the Liturgy of the Hours, what for many centuries was referred to as the "Divine Office." From earliest apostolic times Christians set aside time to pray in the morning and evening, as do many other traditions. Soon Christians started marking off for prayer the third, sixth, and ninth hours as well. Later, by the time of St. Benedict in the fifth century, a more complex pattern of prayer had been established. It involved eight set times each day for prayer. These hours—matins, lauds, prime, terce, sext, none, vespers, and compline—are (with the exception of prime) to some degree the same hours of prayer that are observed in the Liturgy of the Hours today. In a manner similar to the practice of formal meditation or yoga or the recitation of sutras in the Asian traditions or the Muslim *salaat*, the Liturgy of the Hours serves as one of the principal spiritual practices of the Western Church, especially among monastics and other religious.

What we must never lose sight of, however, is the fact that these set hours for prayer are not simply about stopping to pray, but are meant to be an aid to and a reminder of *constant* prayer. In a sense it could be said that they are intended to be a renewal of the prayer that is actually going on all the time. We stop at regular intervals to refresh and renew our constant prayer. This is still at the forefront of the teaching of the Roman Catholic Church in its *General Instruction of the Liturgy of the Hours*, which begins by insisting that constant and persevering prayer belong to the very essence of the Church, the very heart of what it means to be Church—to pray constantly, perseveringly, in praise and in petition, and that this is the whole reason for the Liturgy of the Hours.[1]

The Desert Monks

After Christianity became legalized in AD 313, when there was no longer the chance for martyrdom, some men and women felt they needed to find another way to give themselves totally to God in imitation of Jesus, and so instead of the "red martyrdom" of blood they chose what was called the "white martyrdom" of solitude and silence, and fled to the desert. As Adelbert de Vogue, the well-known Benedictine scholar, tells it,

> The break with the world no longer consisted in defying the law and confronting torture, but in leaving society and living for God alone far from (people) . . . Christ's appeal for continual prayer resounded with more force than ever. Thereafter, to pray without ceasing was no longer to be one of the Lord's directives among others; it was to be the *raison d'etre* of lives freed from every temporal preoccupation . . .[2]

The most famous individual of this era was St. Antony the Great, who is known as the father of monasticism. Saint Athanasius tells us of him that, "Having learned that we should always be praying, even when we are by ourselves, he prayed without ceasing."[3]

There was actually another strand of monasticism also developing at this time, not in the desert but among virgins and celibates and devotees in the cities.[4] However, it is to the desert monks, who left behind an astonishingly rich wisdom tradition, that we will turn for insight into a new and surprisingly radical commitment to prayer, a commitment based literally on St. Paul's admonition to pray constantly. The flight of monks into the desert was to have a lasting influence on Christianity, mainly in that they "considerably sharpened the whole picture, raising the business of commitment to a more dramatic and aggressively challenging plane."[5]

In lower Egypt in the fourth century there were three great monastic centers located south of Alexandria in the Libyan desert:

Nitria, Kellia, and Scetis, the last of which—Scetis—located about sixty-five miles northwest of modern-day Cairo, was the most important. We have two chief sources of information about these monks. The first is the *Apophthegmata*, or Sayings of the Desert Fathers, and the second is the writings of the great John Cassian. Thought to have been born around AD 360 in present-day Romania, John joined a monastery in Bethlehem but then, while still a young monk, went to Egypt with his friend Germanus to learn the science of spirituality from the masters in the desert. Many years after leaving Egypt, John founded two monasteries in what is today France, near Marseilles. It was for those monks that he wrote detailed descriptions of what he had witnessed and learned in the desert. His writings can be found in two collections, *The Institutes* and *The Conferences*. In terms of our subject, the core of these writings—the passage to which many monastic teachers of meditation point again and again—can be found in the latter collection, and it consists of Abba Isaac's two conferences on prayer.

Abba Isaac is an "old man" (a term of respect) of the desert whom John and Germanus have sought out in order to learn about prayer. Abba Isaac passes on to them a formula for contemplation that was handed down to him by the oldest fathers. Abba Isaac says that this formula is sufficient for anyone in any circumstance who wants to have continuous recollection of God. It is simply this: to keep before oneself always the words, "O God come to my assistance; O Lord, make haste to help me" (see Ps 70:1). The reason this particular verse has been chosen from out of all the scriptures is because these words contain

> . . . an invocation of God in the face of any crisis,
> the humility of a devout confession,
> the watchfulness of concern and of constant fear,
> a consciousness of one's own frailty,
> the assurance of being heard,
> and confidence in a protection that is always present and at hand.[6]

What we have here, then, is a short prayer that is presented very much like a mantra. Abba Isaac says that we are to use this as a "formula for meditation, intent on driving every other sort of thought from [our] heart." Like the mantra, this short prayer too is a tool for thinking and involves the use of a "thorn to remove a thorn." Abba Isaac explains:

> Perhaps wandering thoughts surge about my soul like boiling water, and I cannot control them, nor can I offer prayer without its being interrupted by silly images. I feel so dry that I am incapable of spiritual feelings, and many sighs and groans cannot save me from dreariness. I must say, "O God come to my assistance; O Lord make haste to help me."[7]

Abba Isaac then adds that we are to use this phrase to "cast away the wealth and multiplicity of other thoughts, and restrict ourselves to the poverty of this single word." Fr. John Main wrote beautifully about this "poverty" many times, and his closest disciple, Fr. Laurence Freeman, has spoken of it often as well. In meditation we choose the way of poverty, the way of renunciation. We renounce all other words, all other prayers, all other thoughts and, hardest of all, our imaginations and our daydreaming, as we restrict the mind to the poverty of one word or phrase.

Wandering Thoughts: The Monkey Mind

This brief teaching on prayer from Abba Isaac contains such profound insight, especially with regard to distraction in prayer. What are we to do about distracting thoughts, what many Buddhists call the "monkey mind" that is always jumping from this branch to the next, and will never sit still for even a moment? Well, we could try to fight our thoughts and attempt to make our mind stop jumping around by sheer force of will. But that doesn't really seem to work for most people. We get caught up in thinking about not thinking and we end up wasting all our energy trying not to think.

There is another approach, one that is simpler and more effective. It is summed up in Shunryu Suzuki's book, *Zen Mind, Beginner's Mind*, which contains some of the most practical advice on meditation ever put down in words. He notes that when we are meditating we should not try to stop our thinking, but let the thinking stop itself.

If something comes to your mind, let it come in, and let it go out. It will not stay long. When you try to stop your thinking, it means you are bothered by it . . . it is only the waves of your mind, and if you are not bothered by the waves they gradually will become calmer and calmer. In five or ten minutes, your mind will be completely serene and calm. At that time your breathing will become quite slow, while your pulse will become a little faster.[8]

What we do is focus—not on our thinking, on our monkey mind, but on our mantra, our word. We attach our breath, our intention, and our attention to it as if it were a small stone, and we hold onto it as it steadily sinks to the depths. The Buddha said:

As in the ocean's depth no wave is born, but all is still,
so let the practitioners be still, be motionless,
and nowhere should they swell.[9]

On the surface there may be all kinds of little ripples and even big waves (and fallen leaves and old beer cans!), but we want to go below the surface, below the active mind, and, as Jesus says to the apostles, cast "into the deep" (Luke 5:4). So if, as Abba Isaac says, "wandering thoughts" surround us and we have no control over them, or if our prayer seems riddled by distractions, we cling to our mantra.

Orthodox Bishop Kallistos Ware says much the same thing, but adds that in this way our "spiritual strategy" is positive rather than negative: instead of fighting our thoughts directly and trying to eliminate them by an effort of the will, we simply turn and fix our attention somewhere else. Instead of gazing into our turbulent imagination and trying to fight off our distracting thoughts, we look to God. Then the grace that comes through the recitation of our prayer word will overcome the thoughts that we cannot obliterate by our own strength. Instead of trying to empty our minds of bad things, we let them be filled with something we know is good. Two of the other Desert Fathers, Barphinuphius and John, say that we simply "lay before God our powerlessness."[10]

What we are striving for in our prayer is a certain stillness. In the words of the Mahayana Buddhist *Shraddhotpada Shastra*, attributed to Asvaghosha,

While one may at first think of his breathing, it is not wise to continue it very long, nor to let the mind rest on any particular appearances or sights or conceptions arising from the senses, such as the primal elements of earth, water, fire and ether, nor to let it rest on any of the lower mind's perceptions, particularizations, discriminations, moods or emotions. All kinds of ideation are to be discarded as fast as they arise, [and] even the notions of controlling and discarding are to be got rid of. One's mind should become like a mirror, reflecting things but not judging them nor retaining them.[11]

It is simplicity itself; we are choosing the path of utter simplicity when we choose the way of meditation.

Meditation and Contemplation

Throughout this book we have been using the terms "meditation" and "contemplation" interchangeably. At this point it is important to note, however, that there can be distinctions or differences in the ways the terms are used, differences not only between Eastern and Western traditions but also within traditions.

In the Zen tradition, for example, many teachers do not even like to use the word "meditate" to describe *zazen*. But in fact, "meditate" is the usual translation of the original Sanskrit word *dhyana*, which is the root word of the Chinese word *ch'an*, which gives us the Japanese word *zen* (as well as the Korean word *seon* and the Vietnamese word *thien*.) Thus, "meditate" is probably the most fitting translation for what Zen Buddhists do as well.

In the same Asian traditions (Hinduism, Buddhism, perhaps Taoism), "contemplation" is considered a more discursive process. The word "discursive" means "marked by analytical reasoning," or "moving from topic to topic." It might be helpful to think of it as "relating to discourse"—that is, going from one thought to another, the process of expanding on a thought as we would in a speech. We in the West have sometimes used the word "contemplation" in this way, referring, for example, to "contemplating" a beautiful scene of nature or the remembered face of our beloved. More commonly however, in the Christian tradition we have used the word "meditate" to mean that! In the Ignatian tradition, for example, to meditate on Jesus' life or to meditate on Jesus' sufferings means to think about them, to re-create the scenes in our minds, to imagine ourselves in the situations, to note our reactions and surroundings—in a word, to be discursive, to go from one thought to another. This is in clear contrast to the Asian traditions in which, as we have seen, " to meditate" is to go beyond all thoughts and focus single-pointedly on something that will take us beyond all imaginings, a process that, in the West, is usually called "contemplation."

In a sense, "contemplation" in the Western theological sense is our response to God having revealed something to us, but it is a response of being simply present, without thoughts or words. In chapter 6 we will discuss St. John of the Cross's concept of "infused contemplation," contemplation as something that is poured into us, a gift of the Holy Spirit, a grace, something given to us at the end of a journey.

In this book, and for our purposes, I use the word "meditation" in an Eastern sense. The interior journey involves our effort to concentrate so as to be able to meditate and await the gift of contemplation. Meditation is itself "contemplative prayer" in that we hope that through the practice of meditation, through actively learning how and striving to go beyond all thoughts, we will reach a state of contemplation, or perhaps more accurately, a state of being receptive to the gift of contemplation.

Listen to what John Main has to say about meditation and contemplation:

> The word meditation comes from the Latin *meditare* which breaks down into the roots *stare in medio*—to remain in the center. The word contemplation suggests the same. The word contemplation does not mean looking at anything—God or anyone else. Contemplation is being in the temple with God. The temple is your own heart, the depths of your own being.[12]

The temple of our own heart in the depth of our own being is where we are with God, the place where God's Spirit meets our spirit. How apt are the psalmist's words in describing contemplation:

> O God, you are my God, I seek you,
>   my soul thirsts for you;

    my flesh faints for you,
       as in a dry and weary land where there is no water.
    So I have looked upon you in the sanctuary,
       beholding your power and glory. (Ps 63:1-2)

So we need to "stay in the center" because what is there in the center is none other than the temple, and there we will be with God, in the temple of our own hearts. One of my favorite chants that I learned in India is this one, written in the Malayalam language for Pope John Paul's visit to the state of Kerala in 1989.

> *Arati arati ardana!*
> *atmavin shetratil aradana!*
> *angeli angeli prana varchana!*
> *manasa cowelil crede archana!*

Roughly translated it means,

> Adoration! Adoration in the temple of the heart!
> Adoration! Adoration of the mind in the temple of the Spirit!

Contemplation: Staying in the Temple of Our Heart

John Main has this to say about what it means to "stay in the center," in the temple of our heart:

> By meditating we leave all the shallow levels of our life behind and enter into something that is profound. By meditating we leave behind the passing ephemeral things of life and enter into what is eternal. The ultimate goal of all religion is re-linking and it is essentially the re-linking with our own deep center. To be re-linked to our own center is the purpose of all religion. We know from the Christian tradition that the Spirit of God dwells in our own center, in the depths of our own spirit.[13]

Constant prayer, what was taught by the Desert Fathers, is actually the state of being "in the center," in the temple of our hearts. And, turning once more to India, we find a wonderful story that helps illuminate what this means. It is the story of Ramana Maharshi, who was a great Tamilian saint. As a young man he had a death experience that wrought in him a life-transforming spiritual awakening. Here is how he described it:

> "Well, then," I said to myself, "this body is dead. It will be carried to the burning ground and reduced to ashes. But with the death of this body, am 'I' dead? Is the body 'I'? This body is silent and inert, but I feel the full force of my personality and even the sound of 'I' within myself—apart from the body. So 'I' am the spirit, a thing transcending the body."[14]

The sound of "I" is, of course, none other than OM, the sacred syllable of the Hindu tradition. The Maharshi said that, from that moment on, after having this experience, the sound of "I," this OM, was like a *shruti*, or drone sound. In Indian music there is always a drone underlying the melody that comes either from an instrument such as a harmonium or a tambura or from something called a *shruti* box. So the Maharshi's awareness of OM, and of his own essential nature, became like a drone, present throughout all of his life; he was never unaware of his true and essential nature, what we might call his spirit, which was the very ground of his being.

This is an apt image for what we mean when we speak of continual prayer. We long for our awareness of the Spirit poured into the depths of our hearts to be like a *shruti*. We yearn to be constantly aware of the Spirit within us groaning in sighs too deep for words.

In closing our gatherings, my friends and I use a prayer adapted from the Upanishads:

> May our bodies be strong,
> may our tongues be sweet,
> may our ears always hear the sound of your voice,
> O Lord of Love.

The actual line from the *Taitriya Upanishad* is "May my ears always hear the sound of OM, the supreme symbol of the Lord of Love." Through constant prayer we hope to be always aware of the Spirit's song deep in our own hearts.

Questions of Method

One of the best exercises for remaining in a state of constant prayer simply involves awareness of our breathing. This can be done wherever we are, whatever we are doing, with or without a prayer cushion or a set of beads, in a church or in a crowded subway. Once the practice of being intentional and aware of our breathing starts to take root, all we need to do to call ourselves back to mindfulness is to pay attention to our breathing, counting our breaths.

Yashutani Roshi suggests that our breathing should be abdominal, that we need to bring our center of gravity down to the lower abdomen. So, he recommends, you need to imagine that your nostrils are about two inches below your navel! Let your breath flow gently. Try to imagine that you are holding a balloon in your hands, and that you are inflating this balloon with each inhalation. After a while, let the purposeful concern with the inhalations and exhalations just drop away, and let your respiration become natural.

> Except at the beginning of [a period of meditation], when you take a deep breath and then slowly exhale, don't manipulate your breath; allow it to find its own natural passage. Sometimes the breathing will be slow, at other times fast, and at still other times labored, depending on your mind state, your body condition, and other factors, but with continued [meditation] you will develop poise and stability and your respiration will assume its own natural pattern.[15]

The great Zen master Dogen Zenji taught that breathing should neither be grasping nor forced, neither slow nor rapid. He also taught that just the very expansion and contraction of the respiratory muscles involved in abdominal breathing by themselves will soothe and strengthen the automatic nervous system as well as help inhibit the proliferation of random thoughts.[16] It is marvelous to recognize how the body itself can be such a servant and friend to the mind, helping the mind to slow down and focus.

After you have done this for a short time, attach your prayer word or mantra to your breath, and let it set the pace. If you have a word that you have been using and wish to stay with it, please do. If you would like to try a new one, you may want to consider using the phrase that Abba Isaac recommended to John Cassian and Germanus, the phrase that is used in the Roman tradition to begin every celebration of the Liturgy of the Hours:

O God, come to my assistance;
O Lord, make haste to help me.

5

PURE PRAYER

The disciple knocked at the door of the Beloved.
And a voice from within asked: "Who is there?"
The disciple answered, "It is I."
The voice said, "There is no room for two 'I's' in this house."

—Rumi

Then Moses went up on the mountain, and the cloud covered the
mountain. The glory of the LORD settled on Mount Sinai, and the cloud
covered it . . . Moses entered the cloud, and went up on the mountain.
Moses was on the mountain for forty days and forty nights.

—Exodus 24:15–16, 18

In discussing meditation, the inward journey to a place beyond our thoughts and imagination, we have already touched on what is known as "pure prayer." The desert father Abba Isaac uses this term in explaining the importance of utilizing a short phrase—namely, the opening lines of Psalm 70, "O God come to my assistance; O Lord, make haste to help me"—to focus the mind and let go of all else. Out of this poverty one will attain, he says, "that purest of pure prayers which looks for no visual image, uses neither thoughts nor words."[1]

Meditation in the Christian tradition, then, could be thought of as pure prayer, prayer that is beyond all words and images. We might say that it is the prayer of the Spirit praying in us "with sighs too deep for words" (Rom 8:26) when we have united ourselves in our deepest center to that Spirit that has been poured into us.

In his book, *Zen and the Kingdom of Heaven*, Tom Chetwynd states that in the earliest Christian tradition the word "prayer" was used primarily for this type of prayer, pure contemplative prayer. He is not alone in this view. The late well-known Cistercian monk and teacher of Centering Prayer, Basil Pennington, agrees that this was the norm of prayer until the Scholastic era. He adds that since Scholastic times it has been carefully preserved in the Orthodox tradition.

Chetwynd explains that our use of the word "prayer" has come to mean mostly petition, or asking for something. According to him, this is "the lowest form of prayer in the Christian hierarchy" since Jesus himself said, "Your Father knows what you need before you ask him" (Matt 6:8). I myself am uncomfortable with the notion of a hierarchy in prayer and with any tendency toward elitism, because Jesus also often urges us to ask for whatever we want in faith (see, for example, Matt 21:22: "Whatever you ask for in prayer with faith, you will receive"). In addition, there are also other kinds of prayer—prayers of contrition, prayers of silence, prayers of praise and adoration—that Chetwynd does not mention.

Be that as it may, there is no question that by the time of the desert monks there was a clear emphasis on "pure prayer," on praying "without any object in view, without any thought or image in mind."[2] So, in this sense, Chetwynd says, how the monks in the desert prayed was actually what we have been referring to as meditation—"what the Buddha taught, what a Tibetan yogi does, what a Zen monk does." And then Chetwynd goes on to make the very bold assertion that, since the desert monks trace their lineage all the way back to the Gospel, this is what Jesus did, how Jesus prayed—in this pure, objectless way, beyond all thoughts and images.

If we take "prayer" to mean "pure contemplative prayer," and if our "pure contemplative prayer" equals, as Chetwynd says it does, what the Eastern traditions call "meditation," we could then substitute the word "meditation" every time we come across the word "prayer," and "meditate" every time we find the word "pray" in the scriptures. It certainly doesn't work with every mention of prayer in the Gospels, but sometimes it is very moving: "After saying farewell to them, Jesus went up on the mountain to *meditate*" (Mark 6:46). "Now during those days he went out to the mountain to *meditate*; and he spent the night in *meditation*" (Luke 6:12).

The Apophatic Tradition

What this brief introduction to pure prayer now leads us to is a discussion of something called the apophatic way, an approach that for centuries has not been spoken of much in our tradition, at least in Western Christianity. The apophatic way is characteristic of mystical theology, and has been nurtured much more in the Eastern Christian tradition than in the Western.

What do we mean by "apophatic"? Apophatic theology is theology by way of negation. According to apophatic theology, knowledge of God is not a matter of saying what God is like and ascribing certain attributes to God (e.g., God is love, God is light, God is truth) but rather of recognizing that God is totally beyond our ability to understand, to comprehend, to grasp—and certainly to describe. Yes, God is Father, but no, God is not Father as pictured in the old catechisms, an old man with a flowing white beard. Yes, God is person, but beyond any concept, philosophical or otherwise, that we could come up with of "person." So, in the apophatic way, God is known by negating any concepts that might be applied to God, and by "stressing the inadequacy of human language and concepts to say anything about God."[3]

The thirteenth-century Dominican mystic Meister Eckhart went so far as to make such statements as, "God is not wise. I am wise. God is not light. I am light." These things he said got him into a lot of trouble because they were misunderstood. What he was pointing to, however, was the apophatic insight into the fact that all our descriptions of God are hopelessly inadequate. I can be wise—but God is so far beyond anything I could ever be that that word "wise" is hopelessly inadequate when applied to God. All my descriptions are what psychology might call "projections" of qualities I admire onto God.

Cyprian Smith explains it in this way: at some point in every relationship we have to fall out of love with the Beloved projected outside of ourselves, internalize the qualities we have projected onto the other, and find those qualities in ourselves. Then that internalization gradually opens out once more, but this time in a new way. In our relationship with God we move from God "out there" to a realization that God is within us, to a further realization that we are within God. Sometimes the rejection of the religion of our childhood is simply the first stage of what can ultimately be this healthy movement, if we follow it all the way through. "The art is to withdraw the projection with great care and delicacy, so that what emerges at the end is not a hopeless vacuum" of nihilism or despair "but a deeper truth," to strip away the projection in such a way as to reveal the truth that lies behind it, because the Transcendent God "is a truth which can only be revealed gradually by a progressive stripping away of the veils."[4]

The Divine Darkness

Gregory of Nyssa is one of the most influential early Christian writers on this subject. In two of his famous treatises, "The Life of Moses" and the "Commentary on the Song of Songs," he uses Moses' encounters with God as an example of what the human experience of God is like as we grow in faith. Somewhat surprisingly, Gregory teaches that the experience will not be one of increasing light and knowledge, but rather a gradual entrance to more and more divine darkness.

Remember that Moses' vision of God began with light in the burning bush; later on God spoke to him in a cloud: "Then Moses went up on the mountain, and the cloud covered the mountain . . . Moses entered the cloud, and went up on the mountain . . . for forty days and forty nights " (Exod 24:15, 18). As Moses rose higher up Mount Sinai and "became perfect, he saw God in darkness."[5] "Then the people stood at a distance, while Moses drew near to the thick darkness where God was." (Exod 20:21). Gregory writes:

> Now the doctrine we are taught here is as follows. Our initial
> withdrawal from wrong and erroneous ideas of God is a transition

from darkness to light. Next comes a closer awareness of hidden things, and by this the soul is guided through sense phenomena to the world of the invisible. And this awareness is a kind of cloud, which over-shadows all appearances, and slowly guides and ac-customs the soul to look towards what is hidden. Next the soul makes progress through all these stages and goes on higher, and as she leaves below all that human nature can attain, she enters within the secret chamber of the divine knowledge, and here she is cut off on all sides by the divine darkness. Now she leaves outside all that can be grasped by sense or by reason, and the only thing left for her contemplation is the invisible and the incomprehen-sible. And here God is, as the Scriptures tell us in connection with Moses: "But Moses went to the dark cloud wherein God was." (Ex 20:21)[6]

This is the apophatic tradition. It is the roadmap of the journey on which we set out when we meditate, attempting to leave behind all our thoughts about God, and all our images of God—which may actually have become idols that we worship! We hope to be guided through sense phenomena to the world of the invisible, more and more accustomed to look toward what is hidden, to enter within the secret chamber of divine darkness, leaving outside all that can be grasped by sense or reason.

The great Franciscan saint and theologian Bonaventure describes the journey beautifully in his treatise, *The Journey of the Mind to God*:

Seek the answer in God's grace, not in doctrine;
in the longing of will, not in the understanding;
in the sighs of prayer, not in research;
seek the bridegroom, not the teacher;
darkness, not daylight;
and look not to the light but rather to the raging fire
that carries the soul to God with intense fervor and glowing love.
Let us die, then, and enter into the darkness,
silencing our anxieties, our passions,
and all the fantasies of our imagination.[7]

Loss of Self/Emptiness

Bonaventure writes, "Let us die then, and enter into the darkness." What exactly does this mean?

Often in advanced stages of the spiritual life people experience a certain sense of "loss of self" that can perhaps best be described as a kind of death. Let us note, however, that we need to be very careful with our use of that phrase, "loss of self." Spiritual teachers and aspirants often use such expressions as "destroy the ego" or "smash the ego" and, unfortunately, much psychological damage can be and has been done in the name of the subsequent destroying and smashing. So let us proceed with caution.

Abba Isaac tells us that by restricting ourselves to the poverty of a single word, we attain the beatitude "Blessed are the poor in spirit."⁸ What this means is that there is a certain going beyond what we identify as the self—our ego construct, our thoughts, our opinions, all the handles we hold onto to keep us safe in the world—implied in the apophatic way. In Sufism this is known as *fana*, sometimes called the "annihilation of the self" or the "extinguishing of the ego," though here too Muslim scholars say that "annihilation" is not a good translation if it connotes "destruction from above or from the outside." It is probably better to speak in terms of the "gradual dissipation of the self so that the self is forgotten and God [is] remembered."⁹ When the self is forgotten and God is remembered: Ah, that's it! Perhaps this is an experience best expressed in poetry. As Rumi says, "There is no room for two 'I's' in this house."

Thomas Merton referred to *fana* in writing about his own prayer. He said that he had a very simple way of prayer that was centered entirely on attention to the presence of God, God's will and love, and the faith without which no one can know the presence of God.

> One might say this gives my meditation the character described by the Prophet as "being before God as if you saw Him." Yet it does not mean imagining anything or conceiving a precise image of God, for to my mind this would be a kind of idolatry. On the contrary, it is a matter of adoring Him as invisible and infinitely beyond our comprehension, and realizing Him as All. My prayer tends very

much toward what you call *fana*. There is in my heart this great
thirst to recognize totally the nothingness of all that is not God.
My prayer is then a kind of praise rising up out of the center of
Nothing and Silence. If I am still present "myself," this I recognize
as an obstacle about which I can do nothing unless He Himself
removes the obstacle. If He wills He can then make the Nothingness
into a total clarity. If He does not will, then the Nothingness seems
itself to be an object and remains an obstacle. Such is my ordinary
way of prayer, or meditation. It is not "thinking about" anything,
but a direct seeking of the Face of the Invisible, which cannot be
found unless we become lost in Him who is Invisible.[10]

We are speaking of "nothingness" and "emptiness" here, which is scary
territory sometimes for us moderns, accustomed as we are to asso-
ciating such terms with nihilism and despair. It is because we do not
understand this kind of nothingness as actually a fullness that we
sometimes accuse people from Asian traditions of being nihilists.

Catherine de Hueck Doherty, who was herself steeped in Eastern Christianity, has a beautiful passage on this in her book, *Poustinia*. She says that when the French philosopher Sartre, for
example, talks about moving toward nothingness, he really has
nothing. There is nothing behind his nothingness. It's just despair.
As the great Indian philosopher and sage Sri Aurobindo writes,
"the Nihilist's negation of existence is a mere *reductio ad absurdum*
of all thought and reason, a metaphysical *hara-kiri* by which Philosophy rips her own bowels open with her own weapons."[11] But
when Christians move into this "nothingness" we find God. In
Catherine de Hueck Doherty's words:

> There comes a moment in this movement toward nothingness which
> seems to be a moment of nonexistence. It appears idiotic, positively
> idiotic to say such a thing. But it's true. It's a moment in which you
> are nonexistent as far as being a person is concerned. Everything has
> disappeared. You are not even cognizant that "you are." You are only
> cognizant of darkness. Whether you are in depths or heights is un-
> important; you are not even cognizant of that. But there is a moment
> of nonexistence out of which you come. And when you come out,
> prayer begins . . . Now it's a very strange prayer. It's a prayer that
> is no prayer, because it takes place in an *interiorized passivity*. It has

no connection with what you are doing—walking, sleeping, whatever. In you now there is a tremendous change. Prayer now begins to make sense because you don't pray; God prays in you. This is where true liberation enters. Up till now, freedom has been operating. You've submitted yourself to God of your own free will. Now [God] takes over, and that's where true liberation begins.[12]

Now we are back to St. Paul's theology of prayer—in Romans: ". . . the Spirit helps us in our weakness; for we do not know how to pray as we ought, but that very Spirit intercedes with sighs too deep for words" (8:26); and in Galatians: ". . . God has sent the Spirit of his Son into our hearts, crying, 'Abba, Father!'" (4:6).

Neti, Neti! Not This, Not This!

The apophatic approach can serve as a bridge to other spiritual traditions, because we find resonances of it in the mystical language of many traditions. While at first glance Hinduism, for example, appears to be polytheistic, the highest levels of the Indian tradition are expressed in the scriptures known as the Upanishads, which teach that all the deities are actually manifestations of Brahman, the Godhead beyond all name and form. The *Brihadaranyaka Upanishad* uses the famous phrase "*neti neti*," "not this, not this":

> This Self is That which has been described as
> *Neti neti*—"Not this, not this."
> It is imperceptible, for It is never perceived;
> undecaying, for It never decays;
> unattached, for It is never attached;
> unfettered—for It never feels pain, and never suffers injury.[13]

Sri Aurobindo in his *Philosophy of the Upanishads* uses words that could easily apply to the Christian apophatic tradition. The Upanishads distinctly state that neither the mind nor the senses can reach God. Indeed, "words return baffled" from the attempt to describe God.

> . . . we do not discern the Absolute and transcendent in Its reality,
> nor can we discriminate the right way or perhaps any way of teach-

ing the reality of it to others; and it is even held that It can only be properly characterized in negative language and that to every challenge for definition the only true answer is NETI NETI, *It is not this, not that.* Brahman is not definable, not describable, not intellectually knowable. And yet . . . the Upanishads constantly declare that Brahman is the one true object of knowledge and the whole Scripture is in fact an attempt not perhaps to define, but at least in some sort to characterize and present an idea, and even a detailed idea of Brahman.[14]

Abhishiktananda writes in his most famous book, *Prayer*:

Those whose aim is God never stop short at anything, whatever is thought or felt, no matter how exalted or uplifting it may seem to be. God is beyond.

He then goes on to describe how in the Book of Proverbs (30:15-16) it is said that there are three things—and a fourth—that never say "enough!": Sheol, the barren womb, the parched earth, and fire. But, even more than these four, "it is the spirit on its way to God that ceaselessly cries from its own depth: 'not enough!' *'Neti, neti!'*" Nothing can satisfy our spirit, except God's own self. Yet, so long as we are not ready to leave our self behind, we are forever incapable of reaching God. Then only, when we leave our self behind, does our spirit understand that "silence is the highest and truest praise: *Silentium tibi laus* . . ."[15]

The resonance of Christianity with other traditions is of vital importance. Perhaps most authentic religious movements begin with an inspiration, a wordless ecstatic movement of the Spirit in the depths of the heart. But when that movement starts to be described in terms of such things as myth, ritual, and doctrine, then it is that we divide ourselves one from the other—even within our own denominations. This is why meditation can be a marvelous bridge between traditions, because it is an experience before words and concepts, and an experience beyond words and concepts. One of the most successful inter-religious dialogues going on in the world today is that between monks, people who are not arguing about doctrine and dogma but speaking out of their experience of meditation and contemplation, the place before words, the place beyond words.

Would that we could follow Bonaventure's advice to "seek the answer in God's grace, not in doctrine; in the longing of will, not in the understanding; in the sighs of prayer, not in research; seek the bridegroom, not the teacher."

The Death of God

We spoke earlier of Cyprian Smith's insight about the need to "fall out of love with the Beloved." Here, in the words of an anonymous Carthusian monk, is the same insight, but taken to its logical endpoint in relation to God and stated in what might be, for some, shocking terms:

> But you will permit me the risk of saying that
> for all of us God must die at a certain moment.
> In one sense only the atheist can truly believe in God.
> Let me explain:
> it is necessary that the God of our imagination die,
> the God of our projections and desires
> (who is none other than our Ego deified);
> the God who stands alongside the cosmos as some "thing" else,
> who stands alongside the neighbor as someone else,
> in competition with him or her to win my love;
> the God of whom it suffices to know the general moral rules in
>   order to do his will;
> the God infinitely above his creatures' pains in a transcendence
>   beyond reach;
> the God-judge, who punishes in accord with a justice conceived
>   along human lines;
> the God who blocks the spontaneity of life and love.
>
> Such a God must die to make room
> for a God strangely close and familiar
> and nevertheless totally beyond our grasp;
> a God who bears a human face—
> that of Christ, that of my brother;
> who is love in a way that defies all our human notions of justice;
> who is generosity, overflowing life, gratuitousness, unpredictable
>   liberty;

who does nothing "in general,"
but who is always the "You" facing the "I."[16]

At some point all our "gods" must make room for God. Bede Griffiths at the end of his life spoke of how unfortunate it is that we can't find another word for God, because that word is so loaded with all our conceptions. The case is often the same with all our "God language," which comes out of our mouths sounding like so much undigested glop, *quack-quack*.

Rowan Williams, the archbishop of Canterbury, was in New York City on the day of the terrorist attacks in 2001 and later wrote a book called *Writing in the Dust*, a reflection on his experience of that event. In the book he tells us that he read some of the messages sent by passengers on the planes to their spouses and families in the horrible last moments before they died, and he compared them to the spiritual advice that had apparently been given to the terrorists before they embarked on their mission, the kinds of thoughts they were told they should have in their minds as they approached the death they had chosen "for themselves and for others." Rowan Williams notes that "something of the chill of the terrorist attacks of September 11, 2001 lies in the contrast."

> The religious words are, in the cold light of day, the words that murderers are saying to themselves to make a martyr's drama out of a crime. The nonreligious words (of people sending desperate messages to their loved ones) are testimony to what religious language is supposed to be about—the triumph of pointless, gratuitous love, the affirming of faithfulness even when there is nothing to be done or salvaged.[17]

The last thing to note about the apophatic way is that it leads to the prayer that corresponds to the "spirit" in our tripartite anthropology. The Orthodox writer Paul Evdokimov has an intriguing phrase, that this is "an apophatic anthropology leading to an apophatic theology."[18] The anthropology and theology are inseparable. Just as there is a fathomless depth to God, so there is a fathomless depth to us. The mystical tradition and contemplative prayer call us to our own "apophatic depths," to our real and truest self, our own spirit—our real self that is hidden with Christ in God (Col 3:3). Our meditation is apophatic prayer, the prayer beyond our bodies, beyond our minds, beyond our souls, beyond all phenomena, the prayer of *our* spirit and the prayer of the Holy Spirit in sighs too deep for words, the prayer of presence to the God who "dwells in unapproachable light" (1 Tim 6:16).

Questions of Method

Since in this chapter we have been discussing the apophatic way, it seems appropriate at this point to address in greater depth the foundational mantra, OM. We introduced the term in chapter 3, noting that it is an untranslatable sacred syllable. According to Indian philosophy, the most primal reality or sound is *Nada Brahma*, the sound of God, the form of the formless[19]—in a word, OM. Patanjali, who wrote the great Yoga Sutras, says "God's manifesting symbol / is the word of glory OM."[20] And the first and last sound heard by the enlightened is OM. Again, in the words of Patanjali:

> When you worship God with form,
> you must have a name for Him.
> The last word yogis hear before passing into the final condition of
>   illumination is OM;
> when they pass out of it and come to their senses again,
> the first word they hear is OM.
> Call God what you please,
> but OM is God's universal name.[21]

OM is like a threshold sound, the liminal sound. So, when Hindus and Indian Christians begin and end a prayer with OM, they are beginning and ending with what they think of as the God sound, or God-as-Sound. "God spoke it came to be, God commanded, it sprang into being" (see Ps 33:6). What did God say? OM, the Word that is with God, and in some way is God, through which all things come into being.

What do Indian Christians mean when and if they chant the OM? Many, certainly Fr. Bede Griffiths and Abhishiktananda before him, saw a foreshadowing of the Trinity in the sound of OM, which is in actuality three sounds—*A-U-M*—that merge into a single sound. In addition, Abhishiktananda tells us,

> With equal justification we could [also] recognize in the *OM* that Word which eternally proceeds from the silence of the Father . . . It is in that same Word, made human flesh, mind, and word in Jesus Christ, that all our prayer and worship ascends to the Almighty.[22]

Thus, it is not a very far stretch to see specifically the Christ as the Word hidden here in this mantra; one can hardly avoid noting the similarity between the *OM* and the *Logos*-Word of Christianity. In the Christian tradition we speak of Jesus as the Word that God speaks, the *Logos*, and so the Gospel of John begins this way:

> In the beginning was the Word,
> and the Word was with God,
> and the Word was God.
> He was in the beginning with God.
> All things came into being through him,
> and without him not one thing came into being.
> And the Word became flesh and lived among us . . .
>   (John 1:1-3, 14)

In his diary Abhishiktananda translates the prologue of John into Sanskrit: *Agre OM asit . . .*[23]

> In the beginning was the *OM*,
> and *OM* was in Brahman,
> and the *OM* was Brahman.
> All things were made through him and for him . . .
> *OM* was made flesh.

Abhishiktananda then continues to speak of the *OM* resounding everywhere, not only in the Upanishads and in Hindu rituals, but in Christian liturgies and in the Bible, especially in the psalms. In a particularly moving passage he says that *OM* is "the groan of the afflicted, the song of the contented, anger at evil, the fervent appeal, the act of trust, of love."[24] He points out that, even in a Christian interpretation, the *OM* is always "a symbol of God's ineffability," the last step in our journey toward God that is still capable of some kind of outward expression.[25]

The Upanishads teach that

> There are two ways of knowing reality:
> one is through sound and the other is through silence.
> It is through sound that we arrive at silence. (*Maitri Upanishad*
>   6:22)

We are told that the syllable *OM* is the Sound Brahma (*Nada Brahma*) that the body uses like an arrow, with the mind as the point of the arrow, and that the mark is darkness, that which is soundless, immortal, and enduring.[26] In a similar vein, Joseph Campbell explains that the *OM* is made up not just of three syllables but actually consists of four elements:

> What is the fourth element? *A–U–M* and the silence out of which it comes, back into which it goes, and which underlies it. Now my life is the *A–U–M*, but there is a silence that underlies it and that is what we call the immortal.[27]

It is interesting to note that in the Roman Catholic tradition many prayers seem to begin with some form of *OM*: "O my Jesus . . . ," "O my God . . . ," "O my dearest Mother . . ." So, as a concluding meditation to this chapter you may want to choose a short phrase that begins with *OM*. The one that I often recommend to Christians beginning the practice of meditation is simply: "O, my Jesus!"—or "*OM!* My Jesus!"

Or perhaps you may simply choose to immerse yourself in the silence and use the *OM* by itself as the sound of God's self-manifestation deep in the cave of your own heart.

6

THE SOUL'S ASCENT TO GOD

The Tao that can be told is not the eternal Tao . . .
The nameless is the beginning of heaven and earth . . .
The gate to all mystery.

— *Lao Tzu*, Tao Te Ching

Enter through the narrow gate;
for the gate is wide and the road is easy that leads to destruction,
and there are many who take it.
For the gate is narrow and the road is hard that leads to life,
and there are few who find it.

— Matthew 7:13-14

Among the themes that can be traced back to the early years of Christianity, themes that have grown from the tradition of the desert, is that of the three stages of the soul's ascent to God. This is a concept that has its roots in early Neoplatonic thought but stretches right up to—and perhaps even finds its most eloquent expression in—the writings of St. John of the Cross.

Our first source for this concept is the great third-century scholar and theologian Origen. The charge has been made that Christian mystical theology is nothing but baptized Platonism, but it is actually with Origen that we find the first discussions of specifically Christian mystical theology. Origen definitely studied Plato (we know he had the same teacher as the great Neoplatonist Plotinus), but what is important is that Origen studied Plato *as a Christian*. Other great thinkers of the period, such as Justin Martyr or Clement of Alexandria, were converts from philosophy to Christianity, but Origen approached Platonism as a Christian.

Most of the writers of this era, commonly known as the Patristic era, saw the mystical life as nothing other than "the ultimate flowering of the life of baptism," the fruition of our sharing in Jesus' death and risen life by virtue of our having been baptized in water and the Holy Spirit.[1] The same held true for Origen: he viewed the mystical life as simply the working out of Christ's union with the soul, a union that had already been effected in baptism. For Origen, the mystical life was the realization of the already-present communion between God and the soul, and Origen described the unfolding of this communion in language drawn from the great philosopher Plato.

The Three Stages

In the prologue to his commentary on the Song of Songs, Origen writes about how the classical Greek philosophers taught of a threefold ascent of the soul to union with the Divine. The first stage is *ethike*, as in the word "ethics," and has to do with one's manner of life and the habits of virtue. The next stage is *physike*, like the word "physics," and it relates to the inner nature of things, their essential form. Finally there is *enoptike*, a very strange word to us, translated sometimes as "inspective" but roughly meaning the same as metaphysics. As Origen notes, *enoptike* is "that by which we go beyond things seen and contemplate somewhat of the things divine and heavenly, beholding them with the mind alone, for they are beyond the range of bodily sight."[2] There is a sense in which this last stage touches on the apophatic—those things that are beyond the range of bodily sight.

Being deeply rooted in the scriptures, Origen sees the encounter with the Divine as taking place through an encounter with the Word, whom Christians believe to have been made flesh in Jesus. In examining the scriptures Origen finds in them the same threefold path of ascent described by the Greek philosophers. He uses three Wisdom books as examples: the Book of Proverbs, he says, deals with ethics; the Book of Ecclesiastes deals with physics; and finally the Song of Songs is a hymn of "enoptics," or the contemplation of God. In his commentary on the Song of Songs he writes,

> The soul is not made one with the Word of God and joined with
> Him until such a time as all the winter of her personal disorders
> and the storm of her vices has passed so that she no longer vacillates
> and is carried about with every kind of doctrine . . . Then also she
> will hear "the voice of the turtle dove," which surely denotes that
> wisdom which the steward of the Word speaks among the perfect,
> the deep wisdom of God which is hidden in mystery.[3]

Origen also insists on the idea of a progression through three
successive stages. The first stage of the soul's ascent, ethics, has to
do with the formation of virtues. Thus the book of Proverbs char-
acterizes this stage with its practical advice on a virtuous life. By
the time of St. John of the Cross, this stage will be known as the
purgative stage.

The second stage, physics, the stage of "natural contemplation"
or a seeing into the true nature of things, will in time be referred
to as the illuminative stage. This second stage is twofold, with positive and negative dimensions. On the positive side, Origen teaches
that the only way we can know anything of Divine reality is through
some image, some glimpse or trace found in created things. God
has placed in all creatures some hint of invisible and heavenly things
through which the soul can climb to spiritual understanding. We
will see this dimension come to full fruition in Francis of Assisi and
Bonaventure, for whom everything in creation is a sign of the won-
der and love of God. This is natural contemplation, in which the
wisdom of earth leads us to seek the source of that wisdom.

On the negative side, at some point in life we also come to
recognize the transience and futility of all created things. Perhaps
this is why Origen chose Ecclesiastes as emblematic of the second
stage, because the book begins with these lines:

> Vanity of vanities, says the Teacher, vanity of vanities!
>   All is vanity.
> What do people gain from all the toil at which they toil under
>   the sun?
> A generation goes, and a generation comes, but the earth remains
>   forever . . .
> All things are wearisome; more than one can express;
> the eye is not satisfied with seeing, or the ear filled with hearing.

What has been is what will be,
and what has been done is what will be done;
there is nothing new under the sun. (Eccl 1:2-4, 8-9)

Like Plato, Origen thinks that the aim of these first two stages is to subdue the body to the soul, to order the body through the mind. So far, there is no problem, but as we move on we run into a problem area. After the body has been subdued to the soul, we are then to "free the soul from the body," says Origen, echoing Plato. And so for Origen the final stage, *enoptike*—what St. John of the Cross will call the unitive stage—is mainly something the soul looks forward to after death, when the soul becomes *nous* (pure mind or intellect) and is free to contemplate invisible reality.

But we must be very careful with this language about "freeing the soul from the body"! This is Platonic language, not biblical language, and it can easily lead to a tendency to see the body as a "tomb for the soul" as Plato did, instead of as a temple of the Holy Spirit as Jesus did. It can cause us to view the body as an anchor weighing down the soul instead of as an instrument of salvation. Here is where we really need to Christianize our language, and to make sure that we root everything in the Incarnation of Jesus. The flesh is not bad! Otherwise the Word never would have paid it the great compliment of taking it on. Let us never forget that Christianity is based on the fact that Jesus came back from the dead with a glorified body—it was the body that was raised from the dead, and then ascended to the right hand of the Father.

In our modern-day efforts to demythologize the events in the life of Jesus, we might be at risk of throwing out the whole point of the Incarnation! The inner meaning of these stories is that the flesh is made for glory. That's what we celebrate in the Transfiguration of Jesus and in the Assumption of Mary. As St. Paul says, Christ "will transform the body of our humiliation that it may be conformed to the body of his glory" (Phil 3:21). Through our contemplative practice, we are looking forward to being transfigured by sharing in the power of the Holy Spirit. The same Spirit that raised Jesus from the dead is at work in us. *This* is the full flowering of our baptism.

Effort and Grace

While we speak of this path as the soul's ascent to God, we still cannot pressume the grace of union with God, nor can we grab it. The best description of the attitude that we should have during our ascent to God is Paul's description of the attitude of Jesus in the canticle at the beginning of the letter to the Philippians: Jesus did not deem equality with God something to be grasped at, but emptied himself, taking the form of a slave. And it was *therefore* that God raised him on high and gave him the name above all other names (see Phil 2:9).

This is a foundational truth for Christians: there is only so much we can do actively. What this means in practice is clarified by St. Teresa of Avila—a contemporary of St. John of the Cross—when she makes the distinction between what she refers to as consolations and delights. We can actively experience consolation as a result of our practice of prayer and meditation: "We obtain [it] through thoughts, assisting ourselves, using creatures to help our meditation, and tiring the intellect."[4] But there is something beyond consolation—and that is the delight associated with the prayer of quiet, which is infused, which is given. It is a grace. St. Teresa writes, "In the case of this . . . it doesn't come when we want it but when God wants to grant us the favor."[5] Her words may remind us of the distinction we discussed in chapter 4, the difference between meditation and contemplation, and the real meaning of contemplation: meditation is what we do; contemplation is a grace, a gift, something given "when God wants to grant us the favor."

One of the criticisms sometimes leveled against Asian meditation techniques is that they seem to be self-powered cures without any need for Divine grace. But quite often such a criticism is based on our misunderstanding of the doctrines behind these techniques. The workings of grace are spoken of often in Asian traditions as well.

We can find, for example, references to grace in the Yoga Sutras of Patanjali, the most important ancient authority on the spiritual foundation of Yoga. The Yoga Sutras teach that there are eight limbs of Yoga, each one building on the other. The last three limbs deal with meditation proper: concentration, meditation, and absorption (called in Sanskrit *dharana*, *dhayana*, and *samadhi*). The process involves withdrawing the senses from the outside world more and more until a certain one-pointedness is achieved and the individual's attention is fixed entirely within. This brings one to the final stage, *samadhi*, yet it is *samadhi* "with support" (*samprajnata samadhi*), that is, with the support of our own efforts and practice. Beyond that *samadhi* with support there is *asamprajnata samadhi*, or *samadhi* without support, when God is revealed. This is the ultimate, but it is not something that can be grasped; it is a gift, a grace, "when God wants to grant us the favor."

Sri Aurobindo wrote beautifully to one of his disciples about this dynamic between effort and grace: "Within there is a soul, and above there is Grace. That is all you know and all you need to know." He went on to explain that Grace descends and the spiritual life becomes a relationship, like a dance between our effort and grace.

> Without the Grace of the Divine nothing can be done, but for the full Grace to manifest itself the [disciple] must make himself ready. If everything depends on Divine intervention, then man is only a puppet and there is no use of *sadhana* [spiritual practice], and there are no conditions, no law of things—therefore no Universe, but only the Divine rolling things about at his pleasure. No doubt in the last resort all can be said to be the Divine cosmic working under the conditions of Nature. Special intervention there can be and is, but all cannot be special intervention.[6]

Origen too teaches that the soul actively passes beyond what it can by its own efforts, learning the habit of virtue and righteousness, learning the practice of natural contemplation, learning to see the goodness of God revealed in all created reality, and then finally also learning to recognize the futility of all created reality. But then the soul must simply wait, because it can pass through the final stage only by relying on God's mercy. This is the way characterized totally by love, by completely self-emptying love.

Eros

And what is this self-emptying love? Origen calls it "eros," and that is why he spends so much time on the Song of Songs, the Scripture which is emblematic of this stage. In the Christian tradition a distinction has often been made between agape and eros. Part of that distinction reflects our inheritance of Platonic dualism, which was to become Christian dualism. Agape has generally been defined as "good love" (even dictionaries call it "Christian love"), meaning to love as God loves, to love without asking for anything in return. Eros, on the other hand, is generally thought of in terms of sexual and sensuous love—not that there is anything intrinsically wrong with that, obviously, but it often carries a connotation of being somehow lesser, perhaps even tainted. And yet, eros is not just sexual, at least in its original Greek sense; it is so much more. Eros is the love that is a longing, the love that pulls us out of ourselves and draws us to others. As a matter of fact, the ancients talk about our eros for God, and God's eros for us. Dionysius the Areopagite writes in the *Divine Names* that "in God, eros is outgoing, ecstatic. Because of it lovers no longer belong to themselves but to those whom they love."[7] And here is Maximus the Confessor, in "On the Divine Names":

> God is the producer and generator of tenderness and eros . . . God is the moving force in [those] who look to him and [who] possess according, to their own nature, the capacity for desire.[8]

Origen argues that there is no real difference between agape and eros. The love of *enoptike*, the final stage of which we have been speaking, is pure. It is a longing for the invisible, for God, but it is a longing that has been purified. And the first two stages, ethics and natural contemplation, the purgative and the illuminative stages, are the way toward the purification of that love, that eros. At this point we might borrow the language of yoga as Bede Griffiths did and say that eros is transformed into agape.

The first thing we need to do is reverence eros, that primal love of longing, rather than suppress it. The yogic science of the *chakras*, the seven points of energy in the body, would say that we bring the energy up from the first *chakra*, then let it pass through the way of sexuality (the second *chakra*) and be ordered by the way of *ethike*, as Origen might call it, so as to let it be transformed and purified in the third *chakra*, where it is burned and changed into

agape, spiritual love, at the level of the fourth *chakra*. Fr. Bede says
that it is specifically in meditation that we learn to do just that.

> In meditation we can learn to let our own natural desires, our eros,
> awaken and surrender it to God, that is, let it be taken up into agape.
> It must neither be suppressed nor indulged. It is surrender that is
> called for.

Fr. Bede uses even stronger language than this when he goes on to
say that if sexual energy is suppressed, even in prayer—if we fall
into the kind of dualism that denies the Incarnation and views the
body and its primal energies such as sexual energies as bad—then
that energy becomes "neutral or terribly destructive." He concludes
that "there is great danger here which many Christians do not
realize."[9]

Gregory and Evagrius

Returning to our previous discussion of the threefold path, the
three stages of the soul's ascent to God, let us look at two other
major thinkers from the Patristic era who use this image. The first
is Gregory of Nyssa, whose writings on the apophatic tradition we
introduced in the previous chapter. Gregory speaks of the soul's
experience of God as a journey into deeper and deeper darkness,
a journey that involves three stages, which he calls *phos*-light,
nephele-cloud, and *gnophos*-darkness.

The first stage for Gregory is the removal of the darkness of
error by the light of truth, the turning from false reality to God.
Words from a different tradition, the beautiful and well-known
Sanskrit mantra from the *Bridharanyaka Upanishad*, express the
essence of this stage:

> *Asato ma sad gamaya*
> *Tamaso ma jyotir gamaya*
> *Mrtyor ma amrtam gamaya*
>
> Lead me from falsehood to truth,
> lead me from darkness to light,
> lead me from death into life.

The second stage, the way of the cloud, has for Gregory (as the second stage of natural contemplation had for Origen) both a positive and a negative aspect. It is when the soul, looking on created things, learns to see in them a manifestation of the glory of God and, at the same time, their fragility and impermanence, the fact that "all is vanity." One might say that this is when we come to know that all things have a relative existence, that they are totally dependent on the Spirit as their beginning and end.

The third stage is the passing into darkness, into the total incomprehensibility of God. Here there is seeing by not seeing, knowing by not knowing. Insight into this stage seems to be one of the special spiritual intuitions granted to Buddhism, which some refer to as the ultimate apophatic tradition because it refuses to say anything at all about the Divine. This is especially the case after Buddhism meets up with Taoism in China and becomes *ch'an* in China, *zen* in Japan. In the words of the principal Taoist text, the *Tao Te Ching,*

> The Tao that can be told is not the eternal Tao.
> The name that can be named is not the eternal name.
> The nameless is the beginning of heaven and earth . . .
> Darkness within darkness.
> The gate to all mystery.[10]

Gregory of Nyssa's notion of three stages of the soul's ascent to God is mirrored in the teaching of his contemporary, Evagrius of Pontus. Evagrius was a late fourth-century Greek scholar and teacher who became a monk in the Egyptian desert, where he wrote prolifically and was much sought after as a spiritual guide.

Evagrius named the three stages of the soul's ascent *praktike, physike,* and *theologia.* In one of his most famous writings, called *Praktikos,* he lays out what he refers to as the eight *logismoi,* or evil thoughts: gluttony, fornication, avarice, grief, anger, vainglory, pride, and an odd one that is rarely mentioned today called *acedie* or listlessness. The first seven eventually came to be known as the seven deadly sins. According to Evagrius, the practice of virtue involves a battle not so much against the sins themselves as against the evil thoughts that are *unbalanced* passions, thoughts that cause the temptations to sin. What conquering these unbalanced passions leads to is called *apatheia*. That may sound like the word "apathy" but it is not what we understand as apathy. It means more or less a state of tranquility, which Evagrius claims is the natural state of the soul. We know when the soul reaches a state of *apatheia*, because it is able to pray without distraction with the peace that comes from an undisturbed conscience.[11]

St. John of the Cross

Other thinkers would further develop the concept of the three stages of the soul's ascent to God. By the time this concept reached St. John of the Cross in sixteenth-century Spain, the three stages had become known as the purgative, the illuminative, and the unitive. These stages are intimately tied to St. John's teaching about the dark night of the senses and the dark night of the soul, which we find explained in his writings, *The Dark Night of the Soul* and the *Ascent of Mount Carmel*.

The first stage for St. John of the Cross is the purgative stage. Unlike earlier teachers such as Origen, however, St. John views this stage as having both an active and a passive element. We begin by actively purging ourselves of all those things that we know to be against the will of God, all those things that are unhealthy or blatantly wrong. This is the active phase. But then a marvelous thing happens: we stop actively purging ourselves, and a passive purification begins. It's as if we've gotten ourselves so far and then the Spirit of God takes over for us.

At this point, we no longer take pleasure in our old ways, our so-called "worldly ways," yet we are still not experiencing the consolations of the next stage, the illuminative stage. As Henri Nouwen wrote in *The Inner Voice of Love*, it's as if we are about to enter into a new country, but we can't make up our minds about crossing the border. So we cross over and then we come back, and then we cross over again. We feel a little bit of excitement about moving into the new land but we are also filled with fear about leaving behind the old land that we are so used to.[12] Unfortunately, the old land is no longer satisfying, so if we don't take the risk of going forward we will be stuck in a kind of living death for the rest of our lives. This is when the first dark night happens, the transition between the purgative and the illuminative. It is called the "dark night of the senses." This is also the moment of grace; we've done all that we can do and we wait on God to pull us through the rest of the way.

And suddenly grace does appear, and pulls us through, and we experience an illumination—what Origen would say is a knowledge of "the inner nature of things, their essential form." But it does not end there. We are called still beyond. We are called, we might say, into the deeper darkness, into the apophatic depth. St. John of the Cross teaches that at some point we experience a hunger for more, a longing—an eros, if you will—and this too is a working of grace. And so we start then to wean ourselves even of our "religious" consolations. Here is how he describes it:

> Not only must we live in darkness in the sensory and lower part of our nature . . . we must also darken and blind ourselves in that part of our nature which bears relation to God and spiritual things . . . the rational and higher portion of our nature . . . Since this transformation and union is something that falls beyond the reach of the senses and of human capability, the soul must empty itself perfectly and voluntarily . . . of all the earthly and heavenly things it can grasp. It must through its own efforts empty itself insofar as it can. As for God, who will stop Him from accomplishing His desires in the soul that is resigned, annihilated, and despoiled?[13]

So, at this point, we have St. John's famous advice to leave behind all those things we thought of as "spiritual gifts," such as visions and locutions.

> However many supernatural communications we receive, we will continuously live as though denuded of them and in darkness . . . [and] lean on dark faith . . . and rest on nothing of what we understand, taste, feel, or imagine. All these perceptions are darkness that will lead us astray.[14]

Centuries later Bede Griffiths would teach, according to our anthropology of body, soul, and spirit, that all these things—divine

communications, visions, locutions—are in the realm of the soul
or *psyche*, in the realm of phenomena, even if at a very high level.
But they must be left behind to enter into the realm of the spirit,
into the darkness where, as Gregory of Nyssa told us, God is. *Neti,
neti!*—"not this, not that," the Upanishads teach; *nada, nada*—
"nothing, nothing," says St. John of the Cross.

Thus, another purification begins as we move from the illuminative stage to the unitive stage and we begin to wean ourselves of our
spiritual consolations. Again, as in the first purification, this is the
active phase, what we do. But then, at some point, a passive purification begins—this time on a much more subtle level. We can't go
back, and we can't go forward without the movement of grace. Now
the consolations of the illuminative no longer satisfy. In spite of all
the pleasure we once took in religious observances, liturgies and
psalmody, spiritual reading and ascetic practices, there is no longer
any consolation in these things. This is the dark night of the soul.

Note the nature of the "dark nights"—first of the senses, that is,
of the body, and then of the soul! All this before we reach the level
of spirit, and of the Spirit. St. John of the Cross uses Jesus' image
of the "narrow gate and the hard road" from Matthew 7 as emblematic of this way. As Ruth Burrows explains, the narrow gate
is the night of the senses "when we must detach ourselves from
the things of time and sense"; the hard road "relates to the night
of the spirit, and 'few there are who find it.'"[15]

The phrase "dark night of the soul" gets used often and, unfortunately, is probably also often misused. The experience of going
through the dark night of the soul is something that takes place
at a high level of the spiritual life, a level that few people actually
attain.[16] Probably what happens to many people is that they go
through the dark night of the senses, and go through it over and
over and over again, purifying and re-purifying the senses without
actually completing the process and passing beyond.

The Upanishads are always calling us to "train the senses and
still the mind." So, as much as we may, justifiably or not, chafe at
what we perceive to be the moralizing of religion, some kind of
mastery of the senses is required, a proper ordering, so that a right
relationship can be established and so that we may experience

illumination, some knowledge of hidden things.[17] Every authentic spiritual tradition has a way of purification. It must be carried out in a healthy manner, with good psychological balance and self-knowledge, but it must be carried out. Sri Aurobindo tells us,

> I have always seen that there has been really a long unobserved preparation before the Grace has intervened, and also, after it has intervened, one has still to put in a good deal of work to keep and develop what one has got . . . So *tapasya* [ascetical practice, spiritual discipline] of one kind or another is not avoidable.[18]

Questions of Method

At the end of chapter 4 we discussed breathing as a key discipline of meditation. Having pondered in this chapter the ascent of the soul to God, let us look again at breathing, this time not in terms of technique but rather as the sign of the Spirit, empowering us for the journey.

According to the Indian yogic tradition, *pranayama* is the science of breath. *Prana* is thought of as Divine Mother–energy or life force, the universal creative power; and *yama* simply means control. So, the Sanskrit term *pranayama* means control of the life force, control of the Mother-energy within us, by control of the breath.

In ancient times *prana* was understood as the *Atman* itself, the inner self that is one with Brahman, the source of life. *Atman* of course is the Sanskrit equivalent to our own term "spirit." Here is how the late Christian yogi, Swami Amaldas, explained it:

> According to the Bible also *prana* (breath) is closely connected with the Spirit. The word which we translate as "spirit" in the Bible means literally breath . . . "In the beginning God's Spirit moved over the water like a wind" (Gen 1:2). At the creation we are told that God "breathed into (Adam's) nostrils and he became a living soul" (Gen 2:7). Again God revealed himself to Elijah the prophet as a gentle breeze [1 Kgs 19:12]. "Christ breathed his spirit over the apostles" [Jn 20:22]. "The Holy Spirit came at Pentecost like a strong wind" (Acts 2:2).
>
> From this we see how God's Spirit is connected with the breath or *prana*. We experience God's Spirit as *prana* or through *prana*.

Actually *prana* and Spirit go together. In other words, *prana* is the life principle or vital force which sustains our natural life; Spirit is the life principle or vital force of Eternal Life. In the life creation *prana* is manifested as the life force and in the new creation the Holy Spirit is manifested as the life force.[19]

For our meditation as we conclude this chapter, let us begin by once again focusing on the breath that carries this *prana*-life force; and may this make us conscious of the Spirit of God, who hovered over the waters at creation, whom Jesus breathed onto his disciples at Pentecost, and who is blowing in the cave of our own hearts.

Sometimes when all words fail, the mere act of being aware of our breathing may be enough to call us back to prayer, to communion. We might try to simply follow our breath, allowing it to be our mantra, remembering that it is the bearer of the Spirit, and seeing it as the icon of the God beyond all names.

7

PUT YOUR MIND IN YOUR HEART

If when someone leaves their earthly body . . .
they keep the mind in the heart . . .
and, remembering me,
they utter OM, the eternal word of Brahman
they go to the path Supreme.

—Bhagavad Gita 8:12-13

Let your adornment be the inner self with the lasting beauty of a gentle
and quiet spirit, which is very precious in God's sight.

—1 Peter 3:4

In chapter 5 we spoke of the view that pure, contemplative prayer was the norm of Christian prayer until the Scholastic era, and that since that time it has been carefully preserved in the Eastern, or Orthodox, tradition. In this chapter we will be looking more closely at that tradition, seeking in it a bridge not only to our own past, but also to the traditions of the Far East, to Hinduism and Buddhism particularly, because it speaks often of a similar practice and experience of interiority in Christian language.

We will be drawing from two main sources. One is the famous *Philokalia*, a collection of writings by the Fathers of the Eastern Church from the fourth through the fourteenth centuries. It was compiled in Greek in the eighteenth century, subsequently translated into Slavonic, and then translated into Russian by the great Bishop Theophan the Recluse. To this single book is attributed much of the credit for the rebirth of monasticism and the practice of the Jesus Prayer in Russia. The other book is less well known; it is called *The Art of Prayer* and is a spiritual anthology drawn from the Greek and Russian traditions. Compiled by a Russian Orthodox monk named Igumen Chariton, *The Art of Prayer* includes extensive quotations from Theophan the Recluse, translator of the *Philokalia*, as well as other authors.

Something else that has been preserved and handed on by the Eastern Christian tradition is the anthropology that serves as a foundation for this book—namely, the view of the human being as body, soul, and spirit. This anthropology has been articulated clearly and often by Eastern writers.[1] Theophan himself, for example, in *The Art of Prayer* notes that

> the body is made of earth; yet it is not something dead but alive and endowed with a living soul. Into this soul is breathed a spirit—the spirit of God, intended to know God, to reverence Him, to seek and taste Him, and to have its joy in Him and nothing else.[2]

The distinction between soul and spirit is not always easy to understand. Here is one way of explaining it: the soul is the basic principle of life; the soul is what makes a human being something alive, as opposed to an inanimate mass of flesh. The soul is "the form of the stuff." But the soul still exists primarily on the natural plane. It is the spirit that brings us into contact with Divine realities on the spiritual plane; the spirit is the highest faculty in human beings; the spirit is that which allows us to enter into communion with God; the spirit is the soul of the soul. Our spirit is closely linked with God's Spirit, the Third Person of the Trinity, the Holy Spirit. Orthodox writers frequently warn us to remember that the two are not identical, and that confusing them or conflating them would be to end in a kind of pantheism, but nevertheless the fact remains that they are closely related.

The body, the soul, and the spirit all have their own special way of knowing: the body learns by gathering information through the senses; the soul learns through use of the intellect, through reasoning, through thinking; the spirit learns through a mystical perception, by means of intuition that transcends our ordinary consciousness and rational processes.

The Heart

Building on this anthropology, this view of human nature, the Orthodox tradition adds another important element, or perhaps better, another important image, that is, the *heart*. Especially since there has been a certain lack of consistency in philosophical language regarding the third element, which we have been calling the "spirit," in the end, as Tomas Spidlik notes, "Christian writers returned to the language of Scripture and of the people: it is the heart, with which the Spirit is linked, which is 'the seat of the Spirit.'"[3]

Usually when we speak of the heart in contemporary Western society we mean the emotions and affections. But, as Bishop Kallistos Ware points out, "in the Bible, as in most of the ascetical texts of the Orthodox tradition, the heart has a far wider connotation."[4] The heart is the principal organ not just of our physical being, but also of our psychological and spiritual being. And so in the Orthodox tradition we find references to the heart of the body, the heart of the soul, and the heart of the spirit.

The heart exists on the material level, obviously; it is a part of our body, the center of our physical organism. Bishop Kallistos says this shouldn't be forgotten: "When Orthodox ascetic texts speak of the heart, they are not speaking in a purely symbolic or metaphorical sense; they mean among other things the carnal heart, the muscle itself."[5] Then, in addition, the heart is connected in a special way with our psychic composition, with our psyche, that is, our soul. If the heart stops beating, for example, we know that the soul is no longer in the body. But, most important of all, especially when we are dealing with prayer and meditation, the heart is linked to the spirit, to *our* spirit. In the words of Theophan the Recluse,

> the heart is the innermost [person], or spirit. Here are located self-awareness, the conscience, the idea of God and of one's complete dependence on [God], and all the eternal treasures of the spiritual life.[6]

Thus, the heart means the "inner person" to which St. Paul refers. The First Letter of Peter also contains a beautiful passage that speaks of "the inner self with the lasting beauty of a gentle and quiet spirit [*pneuma*] . . ." (1 Pet 3:4). Theophan calls this "the

God-like spirit" that was breathed into Adam in Genesis, that "remains with us continuously, even after that Fall."[7] Bishop Kallistos says that this use of the term "heart" is also what the Rhineland mystics such as Meister Eckhart or the Flemish mystics such as Ruusbroek call the *grunt* or "ground" of the soul where we come face to face with God.

The Mind in the Heart

Prayer, according to Theophan the Recluse as quoted in *The Art of Prayer*, is "standing before God with the mind in the heart." As long as we pray with our mind in our head, as long as we depend solely on our intellectual resources, we are never going to be able to have an immediate, personal encounter with God. And that is our goal. We need to move from our mind to our heart, from knowledge to love.

It is important to note that what we are talking about here is not necessarily romantic, affectionate love, but that deepest love which is the stirring of our inmost essential being. (Remember our discussion of eros earlier. Love may be erotic—read the writings of the Carmelites!—but eros is pre-sexual and a lot more than sexual as well.) Neither are we talking about the surrender of our reasoning faculties to our emotions, which would lead to a condition often seen today, a sort of "tyranny of the affect" in religion.

We are more than just emotional beings. We are also intellectual beings, and our minds and our rationality help us. We need to use our rationality, but we can't stay in our heads either. Our reasoning faculties, our intellects, our minds are just tools; they are not ends in themselves. As a matter of fact, the mind itself can and often does become a trap: we can spend so much time thinking about God, and intellectualizing and discoursing about God, that we fail to actually know God. This is often a danger for "professional religious."

As we move from knowledge to love, we carry our knowledge with us. In the words of Bishop Kallistos Ware, "we are called to descend not *from* but *with* the intellect. The aim is not just 'prayer of the heart,' but 'prayer of the intellect [or mind] in the heart' . . ."[8]

The Three Degrees of Prayer

Building on the tradition of the "prayer of the heart," Theophan the Recluse formulates a beautiful teaching on the three degrees of prayer, corresponding to the heart of the body, the heart of the soul, and the heart of the spirit—which is "the heart of hearts."

The first degree of prayer, bodily prayer, can consist of reading, standing, prostrations—all our liturgical prayer, for instance—but especially for our purposes it means oral prayer, the prayer of the lips. It means the recitation out loud of a word or phrase.[9] According to Theophan, however, the power is not in the word or words themselves but rather in the thoughts and feelings (note how this differs significantly from the notion of the mantra).

The second degree of prayer is prayer with attention: the mind becomes accustomed to gathering itself, re-collecting itself at the time of prayer, and it prays consciously throughout, without distraction. If the prayer involves written words—reading scripture or chanting or reciting psalms or other prayers—the mind is so focused on those words that one reaches "the point of speaking them as if they were [one's] own." Theophan calls this "the union of prayerful thoughts and feelings with the mind and the heart." In the case of a prayer word, such as a mantra, the word has ingrained itself into the mind in such a way that it has become fully internalized. It has gone from the lips to the mind. But the power is not in the thought itself, just as it was not in the words themselves; the prayer is in the thought combined with feeling; real prayer happens when we have placed the mind in the heart.[10]

The third degree of prayer is referred to by Theophan in one passage as the "prayer of feeling," when the heart is warmed by concentration, when what has been spoken and thought is now felt, when we pass from action and thought to true feeling. We enter into the prayer of feeling when we have put the mind in the heart or, as the Upanishads say, into the *guha*, the "cave of the heart," the room or inner chamber of which Jesus spoke (see Matt 6:6). This is also the place of continuous prayer, unceasing prayer, where the prayer prays itself. Now it is, Theophan says, that spiritual prayer begins: "This is the gift of the Holy Spirit praying for us, the last degree of prayer which our minds can grasp."[11]

Here we have come almost full circle: what the Christian scriptures teach is that the Holy Spirit is inside of us praying. Paul says
that the Spirit is saying "Abba! Father!"—the very prayer of Jesus—
that the Spirit is in us, praying "in sighs too deep for words." So to
put our mind in our heart really means to unite ourselves with
Jesus' own prayer, the prayer of and in the Spirit.

Theophan's three degrees of prayer correspond to something
we have touched on many times already: our prayer word or mantra "may go with the first two [degrees], but its real place is with
unceasing prayer."

> You must pray not only with words but with the mind,
> and not only with the mind but with the heart,
> so that the mind understands and sees clearly what is said
>   in words,
> and the heart feels what the mind is thinking.
> All these combined together constitute real prayer,
> and if any of them are absent
> your prayer is either not perfect,
> or not prayer at all.[12]

We also find in Theophan a distinction made by other mystical
writers, a differentiation between active and passive, between what
Theophan calls "strenuous" and "self-impelled" prayer. When prayer
is strenuous we strive for it, we offer it by means of our own conscious effort. When prayer is self-impelled, the prayer offers itself
spontaneously, having been bestowed on us as a gift. (Note that it
is *the prayer* that is self-impelled; it is not *we* who are self-impelled!)
This distinction is reminiscent of our comments in chapter 4 about
the difference between meditation and contemplation, and of the
distinction St. Teresa makes between consolations and delights.

"Self-impelled" prayer, contemplation, delights—whatever it is
called, this type of prayer is given as a gift. It may come to us from
time to time or it may be unceasing. In either case it is prayer that
continues within us no matter what we are doing, whether we are
walking or talking, working or playing, sleeping or awake. It prays
itself. This is the *sahaja samadhi* (the highest state, beyond both
action and contemplation) of which Bede Griffiths spoke, the

shruti or drone of the OM described by Ramana Maharshi—it is when prayer is no longer a series of acts we do, but a state of being.[13]

Put in simple terms, the technique of prayer and meditation is a matter of putting the mind in the heart, going from the body through the soul into the spirit. The prayer begins verbally, on the lips, corresponding to one's physical heart, the heart of one's body. It then becomes ingrained in the mind, which, having internalized the prayer, repeats it on its own; this corresponds to the heart of one's soul. But the ultimate goal is "to put the mind in the heart," to allow one's consciousness to go home to one's spirit, to the inner chamber of one's being, and there to be flooded with the love and light of God. Meditation, yoga, breathing exercises, running, reading, chanting all lead to this: putting the mind in the heart, reintegrating one's being—body, soul, and spirit.

There is a devotional prayer that I was taught to pray as a child before the gospel is proclaimed: "Lord, be in my mind, on my lips and in my heart that I may receive your holy Word," blessing each of those spots on the body with a sign of the cross. At the risk of being an unscrupulous modifier of tradition, I have consciously changed it to remind myself always of the pattern: "O Lord be on my lips, in my mind and in my heart, that I may receive your holy Word," that the Word may go from my lips into my mind, and from my mind sink into my heart.

The Jesus Prayer

An entire volume of the *Philokalia* is devoted just to writings on the prayer of the heart. This type of prayer is known by various names—perhaps most popularly as the Jesus Prayer, since for centuries the mantric prayer typically used by Greek and Russian monks has been some form of "Lord Jesus Christ, Son of the Living God, have mercy on me." It is also known as "hesychast" prayer. Hesychasm is the tradition of inner mystical prayer dating from the fourteenth century and associated primarily with the monks of Mt. Athos in Greece. (The Greek word *hesychia* means "quietness.")

Fr. Bede Griffiths said that he had prayed the Jesus Prayer for many years himself, which was surprising since he rarely spoke of the Eastern Christian tradition in this regard. He compared the Jesus Prayer, the prayer of the heart, with what is written in the *Bhagavad Gita*:

> If when someone leaves their earthly body
> they are in the silence of Yoga
> and, closing the doors of the soul,
> they keep the mind in the heart
> and place in the head the breath of life
> and, remembering me,
> they utter OM, the eternal word of Brahman
> they go to the path Supreme.[14]

Fr. Bede made the comment that this is how one should prepare to die, by closing the gates of the body, by closing the gates of the senses, adding that one should "'hold the mind within the heart,' or as the Greek Fathers say, 'Lead your thoughts from the mind into your heart.'"

> One should sit and meditate and withdraw the mind from the senses, then withdraw the inner mind from the movements of the mind . . . Finally one should withdraw into the inmost center of one's being and then, as everything else drops off, one enters into that eternal *samadhi*.[15]

In fact, this is how Fr. Bede did die. At the commemorative event at Shantivanam marking the centenary of his birth, Sr. Mary Louise, who had tended to him in his final days after he had had a series of strokes, told this story:

> . . . we all know that Bede prayed the Jesus Prayer for over forty years, but none of us heard him formulate it. Well, this was the moment. All of a sudden I heard "Lord Jesus Christ, have mercy on me" (pause) and the right hand beating the chest "a sinner . . ." and from that day onwards, each time I saw the prophet, in tears—struggling—nervous—exhausted in that bed I would just pray: "Lord Jesus Christ, Son of God, have mercy on me" (pause). I would remain silent and Bede beating his chest would say "a sinner." Everything would settle for some moments and then all had to begin anew.

So, we descend into the heart. And there, in our inner chamber, we discover the "godlike spirit" that the Holy Spirit implanted in us when we were created, and with that spirit we come to know the Spirit of God. This is why we say that we have to return to ourselves if we are going to learn this way of prayer.

Remembrance

The prayer of the heart is often compared to Yoga—much to the chagrin of some Orthodox believers—because it involves a physical technique both of posture and of breathing, which we will discuss in the final section of this chapter. But the prayer of the heart is also sometimes linked with Sufism, the mystical branch of Islam, and particularly with the Sufi practice of *dhikr*, or remembrance. Here is one description of *dhikr* from the book *Beads of Faith*:

> There are three stages of *dhikr*: firstly, recitations are purely verbal; secondly, heart and tongue unite to open the seeker's heart through the Supreme Name; finally, *La ilaha illallah* is attained, where there is no reality except God. The ultimate achievement is *fana fi Allah* (the extinction of the self in God).[16]

Thus, first comes verbal recitation with the tongue in mantric fashion. The most popular phrase in Islam would be *Allahu akbar* (God is great), or one of the ninety-nine beautiful names of God, or certain short verses from the Qur'an to help the mind chase out mundane thoughts and distractions and begin to concentrate on God. Then comes remembrance of the heart, which is more profound, inward meditation, shifting from a repetition of spoken words to thoughts. And finally comes what is called "remembrance of the secret," when the person praying is at the center of his or her being, the place of immediate vision of God. "Here there is effortless thought of God; the Sufi is in God and God is in him [or her]. Ecstatic union has been reached."[17]

Specifically regarding our theme of "putting the mind in the heart," listen to the explanation given by the great eleventh-century Sufi mystic Al-Ghazali:

In general how is a mystic way . . . described? The purity which is
the first condition of it . . . is the purification of the heart completely from what is other than God most high; the key to it, which
corresponds to the opening act of adoration in prayer, is the sinking
of the heart completely in the recollection of God; and the end of
it is complete absorption (*fana*) in God.[18]

Al-Ghazali goes on to say that this is the "end" relative to those
first steps—purification of body and of heart—but it itself is really
the first step of the mystic way. Note here the similarity to our
threefold path of the soul's ascent: first purgation and the dark
night of the senses; then illumination followed by the dark night
of the soul; and finally union, which Islam speaks of as absorption
into God—*fana*.

Questions of Method

The type of prayer we have been discussing is mystical, and in our
approach to such prayer it would be easy lose our moorings. This
is why techniques of posture and breathing are so important. To
be honest, many Christian authors on meditation do not place
much emphasis on such techniques. (With regard to posture, Fr.
Bede Griffiths often said he meditated best reclining.) Nevertheless, the physical discipline required for proper techniques of posture and breathing are commonly understood to have important
effects not only on the physical and mental level but also on the
spiritual level.

Meditative techniques are meant to prepare and predispose us
physically and mentally for our spiritual practices. As for posture,
the ultimate goal of Yoga in its classical context, for instance—when
it is about more than athletic stretching and flexibility—is "to prepare [us] for the acquisition of that repose of spirit necessary for
the realization of the 'Supreme,' or for 'experiencing the Divine.'"[19]
The postures are not ends in themselves; the postures are about
predisposing us to have an experience of the spirit, training the
senses and stilling the mind so that our real true nature can shine
through. And our real nature, as Evagrius said, is *apatheia*—peace,
tranquility. According to Simeon the New Theologian,

Our mind is pure and simple, so when it is stripped of every alien thought, it enters the pure, simple Divine light and becomes quite encompassed and hidden therein, and can no more meet anything there but the light in which it is.[20]

As for breathing, by exerting physical control over it we slow the body down and in doing so we allow it to heal itself in many different ways. Breathing exercises are especially good for the heart. On a mental level, breathing exercises can simply clear the mind and be an aid to concentration and gentle exertion, training the mind to be single-pointed and at rest, to drop below the tumultuous thoughts that dart about in our heads to a place of stillness.

But the most important effect is spiritual, because a still mind can allow the inner light of the spirit to shine through and direct our thoughts, words, and actions. Swami Muktananda says, "We do not meditate only to relax a little and experience some peace. We meditate to unfold our inner being." The Eastern Fathers also spoke of a method of breathing that aided the spirit. Nicephorus the Solitary, for instance, writes:

And so, having collected your mind within you, lead it into the channel of breathing through which air reaches the heart and, together with this inhaled air, force your mind to descend into the heart and to remain there. Accustom it . . . not to come out of the heart too soon, for at first it feels very lonely in that inner seclusion and imprisonment. But when it gets accustomed to it, it begins on the contrary to dislike its aimless circling outside, for it is no longer unpleasant and wearisome for it to be within.[21]

To close this chapter, with our posture and our breath aligned and providing us with a suitable ambience for prayer, let us use for our mantra the hesychast prayer, the traditional Jesus Prayer: "Lord Jesus Christ, Son of the Living God, have mercy on me."

8

LECTIO DIVINA
AND THE BEAUTIFUL NAMES OF GOD

Through belief in the Name
the mind soars high into enlightenment,
and the whole universe stands self-revealed . . .
Such is the power of God's stainless Name.
Those who truly believe in it, know it.

—Guru Nanak

In the beginning was the Word,
and the Word was with God,
and the Word was God . . .
And the Word became flesh and lived among us,
and we have seen his glory
the glory of a Father's only son,
full of grace and truth.

—John 1:1, 14

Each of the previous chapters addressed some aspect of the object of our meditation and concluded with a section on questions of method. Having laid this groundwork, we will in this final chapter sum up our work by combining considerations of both object and method in a reflection on two tangible, practical ways of fostering the practice of mediation: *lectio divina* and the "beautiful names of God."

Lectio Divina

Lectio divina means simply "holy" or "divine reading."

When I teach the Liturgy of the Hours, which is the official prayer of the church, I make it a point to begin by explaining to my students that my ultimate goal is *not* to help them to learn how to pray this official prayer of the Church. My goal is to help them (and myself), in the words of St. Paul, to pray constantly or, put another way, to live prayerfully.

The best way to accomplish that—constant prayer and prayerful living—is to pause every now and then, to stop whatever we are doing and re-establish conscious contact with God, what the Sufis call *dhikr*, "remembrance" of God. And when we stop, one of the best things we can do is spend some time with sacred scripture, not studying it as if it were a textbook or a history book, but immersing ourselves in it, treating the experience as an encounter with the living God, seeing the words of scripture as God's words spoken to us, because we believe this is what they are. In the ancient desert the monks sat reading the psalms and other passages from scripture to themselves and to each other day after day—not primarily to pray to God, but first to *listen* to God. Even the psalms were seen not as their words spoken to God but as God's words spoken to them. This is the particularly monastic approach to scripture.

In choir, for instance, as I listen to my sisters and brothers chanting the psalms back and forth, I am aware that these are not our prayers to God as much as they are God speaking to us, and what we are doing is proclaiming God's Word out loud to each other. Our prayer takes place in the silence after the readings. In the ancient desert communities, perhaps all the brothers would be sitting around braiding palm fronds into baskets to keep their hands busy and their minds from drifting while one of the brothers would read a psalm or another scripture text out loud. And when that reading was finished all would stand and raise their arms in the form of a cross and pray, perhaps murmuring to themselves, perhaps silently in their hearts. That is when their prayer took place—in response to the Word of God.

In general we all need some content to our prayer. This is what Swami Muktananda would refer to as the object of our meditation, our intention, our knowing why and on what we are meditating. For us as Christians, the best way to set this intention is through an encounter with God's Word. The setting for this encounter doesn't have to be as elaborate as the whole Roman Liturgy of the Hours or even the eucharistic liturgy, though it certainly could be.

When I lead a meditation session, for example, I always organize it in such a way that we begin by listening to scriptures, not just our own but also those of other faith traditions. Then we say some introductory prayers to focus our intention; this is followed by the chanting of one or a few psalms (the pre-eminent hymns of the Judeo-Christian tradition) and the reading of a short passage from the Christian scriptures, all to focus our intention, to give us something to grab onto, some reminder of our purpose. Even this may be too elaborate for some individuals, but I have found over and over again that people—and I myself—need these kinds of sacramental elements to call us home, to bring us in from the outside to the inside. This is especially true for people who are coming to prayer and meditation after a busy day, perhaps having just been caught in traffic or worn out from dealing with work or family problems.

There may of course be some people who do not require any kind of input, or who have grown beyond the need to use scriptures, but I think they are quite rare. Given the human condition, there is always the danger of solipsism in the spiritual life, the risk of getting caught up in and locked into our own worldview. We need to have a healthy respect for the weakness of our egos. We need to recognize that "going it alone," without any reference to the wisdom that surrounds us and has gone before us, without any kind of objective guide to lead us through the labyrinth of the inner world, means journeying on a path that is fraught with traps and slippery slopes.

When choosing the object of our meditation, pride of place is given to scripture. In addition, though, there is a long tradition of other types of reading (of devotional or spiritual books or of poetry) and other types of experiences (listening to music, looking at art) that can serve the same purpose. At times we read academically, to learn facts and figures, dates and names, or we listen to music or look at art critically, analytically. *Lectio divina*, however, is totally different. It is gentle, like reading a love letter, or hearing a loved one's voice, or gazing on a loved one's face.

Lectio is actually the first stage of a four-fold process that comprises *lectio, meditatio, oratio, contemplatio*—that is, reading, meditation, prayer, contemplation. This pattern summarizes everything we have discussed in the preceding chapters.

After we have read (*lectio*) a small portion of scripture, perhaps two or three times, we then meditate (*meditatio*) on what we have read, but this is meditation in the traditional Western sense, meditation as discursive thought. It is not wordless meditation, which is here called *contemplatio*, and which comes at a later stage. The most famous image of *meditatio* is *ruminatio*, to ruminate. Much like a cow chews her cud, so we chew on the Word, drawing out of it all the meaning it contains. Another famous image often used for *meditatio* is based on a gospel phrase: after Jesus' birth, when the shepherds go to the manger in Bethlehem and make known what the angels have said about this child, we are told that Mary kept all these things and "pondered them in her heart" (Luke 2:19). We have already mentioned that *lectio* is like reading a love letter. *Meditatio* would be like savoring every single word of the letter. We might read it once really quickly, and then read it again more slowly, paying attention to every word. What did she mean when she said this? What did he mean by that? Then we might go back to the letter two or three times to more deeply appreciate a turn of phrase or to steep ourselves in the experience of closeness with the writer, our loved one.

Meditatio leads to *oratio*, or prayer, which is our response. There are many forms this *oratio* could take, but I would like to offer an example particularly suited to our purposes here. Years ago, during my first years in the monastery, we young monks were urged to do our *lectio divina* each morning on the readings of the day, especially on the gospel that would be proclaimed at Mass. One of my friends developed the practice of reading and meditating and condensing and simplifying until he came up with the shortest prayer possible drawn from the reading, a word or a short phrase that would serve as a sort of emblem for the reading, a reminder of the message contained in the passage, the pearl of great price, the treasure hidden in the field. He would then write that prayer word or phrase on a little piece of paper and carry it around in his pocket all day. It would become his mantra for the day.

I believe that this practice captures the purpose of the mantra, especially as Thomas Keating speaks of it. The "word" is a summary of our intention, a tangible reminder of our moment of intimacy with God, like a wedding ring or an amulet worn around the neck. The ancient Hebrews engaged in such a practice, as do modern Orthodox Jews who take quite literally the admonition in Deuteronomy:

> Keep these words that I am commanding you today in your heart. Recite them to your children and talk about them when you are at home and when you are away, when you lie down and when you rise. Bind them as a sign on your hand, fix them as an emblem on your forehead. (Deut 6:6-8)

Thus, the root of our mantra is in the Word. And then that prayer word, the mantra that comes out of our *lectio, meditatio,* and *oratio,* is—to use John Main's marvelous phrase—meant to lead to the silence of *contemplatio*. (His first and most famous book is entitled *Word into Silence*.) This word begins on our lips, goes to our mind, and finally becomes part of us as we "put our mind in our heart."

The movement toward ever-greater simplicity is reminiscent of the advice given in the *Cloud of Unknowing* on using as few words as possible in prayer, and of Abba Isaac's instruction on restricting oneself to the poverty of a single word. Here is André Louf, writing on the psalms:

> It can happen that the psalmist returns to silence and . . . prefers to remain there. It is perhaps this that at length must happen . . . Such an evolution should not surprise us. Over time, the variety of the words of the Psalter is no longer necessary, not because they are now dead weight, but because they have already borne their fruit. They have condensed themselves into a few words, at times into one word only, but a fundamental word, one of those infinitely ruminated words in which one summarizes all the "good news" of salvation and the whole of humanity's response in prayer. From the decachord (the "ten stringed lyre," cf. Ps. 92:4), which was at the beginning, the song of the prayer has become a monochord. Eventually this can find its fulfillment only in that sacred monotony that incessantly shows forth the one thing necessary: the tenderness of God.

The silence then becomes praise. And if a word still remains, only the Name of Jesus our savior will suffice, the blessed Name, untiringly invoked, of the one who is entirely to the praise of God the Father (cf. Phil 2:11).[1]

And so, in the end, my prayer word leads to silence, my mantra helps me to "put my mind in my heart" and draws me to the still waters deep in my being beneath the waves and ripples on the surface, to this last stage of *lectio divina*—*contemplatio*, waiting for the grace of contemplation, when I shall see God face to face.

The Beautiful Names of God

The breath that does not repeat the name of God is wasted breath.

—Kabir

The most beautiful mantras of all, of course, are any of the names of God. Muslims have a tradition reciting one of the ninety-nine beautiful names of God with a set of beads called a *tasbih*, associated also with the Sufi practice of *dhikr.* There are different forms of *dhikr*, or "remembrance," that "suit specific occasions and times of day (before sleep, on waking, at midday, after the five daily prayers), and they may be accompanied by meditation on verses from the Qur'an" as in our own *lectio divina.* But mainly *"dhikr* involves reciting God's ninety-nine names or, with the permission of a *shiekh*, the word *Allah* while using the *tasbih* so that the Divine quality within each Name induces a God-absorbed spiritual state." Other phrases that might be used in the repetitions are phrases such as *La ilaha illallah* (There is no god but God); *Subhana'llah* (Glory be to God); *Alhamdulillah* (All praise is due to God); *Allahu akbar* (God is great); and *Astaghfiru ilah* (May God forgive me).[2]

Muslim practice is particularly relevant in this context because, as George Maloney has pointed out, the physical aspect of the hesychast method, which we discussed in chapter 7, seems to have been influenced by Muslim mysticism, which in turn was influenced by Hindu and Buddhist mysticism.[3] In Muslim practice, the penitent tries, by focusing all the attention on one part of the body or upon some object, and by repeating a sacred name or word, to synchronize the breathing with the spiritual movements of the soul, gradually moving into the interior depth of one's being, the core or center of one's existence, and there uniting oneself with God. Though Maloney does not think this is essential to true hesychasm, there are clearly universal resonances to be found, and they are quite striking.

From India comes the practice of *nama japa*, which means simply, "repeating the name." In our ashram in South India, the last prayer of the night takes place just before sleep when the monks gather in the temple, close the doors of the tabernacle area and sing, *Yesu, Yesu, jai, jai! Namo! Yesu, Yesu, jai jai! Namo!*—"Jesus, we praise you, we bow to you!"—over and over again. Ram Dass teaches that according to *bhakti* yoga, the yoga of devotion, the Name of God is no different from God's own self. Even if we cannot know who or what God really is, through our loving devotion and through *bhajan* (remembrance) of the Divine Name, "it seems that we can draw the One towards us in the same way as a child left alone in the dark room brings its mother with its cries." Ram Dass writes:

> Chanting the names of God is a *sadhana*, a spiritual practice that utilizes both the body and the mind to bring us to the feet of the Beloved. Through singing and hearing the Name, the mind is gently brought to a state of concentration.
>
> The mind dwells on what it covets. A greedy person will be thinking of money and how to get more of it, but the lover of God longs only to be in "the presence." What begins as a faint spark is fanned into a flame of ecstatic awareness by the repetition and remembrances of the Name. The *kleshas* [impurities of the mind-body] are burnt in this flame and when there is no dust left on the mirror of the mind, truth is reflected there.[4]

Muslims, Hindus, and Christians tend to want to personalize the word as an act of devotion. We find this tendency also in the Buddhist Pure Land tradition, in which the most prominent spiritual practice is called the *nembutsu*, which means "mindfulness of the Buddha." During the earliest period of this form of Buddhism, practitioners used a type of meditation that involved meditating on the Buddha and his merits. This gradually evolved into a visualization of the Buddha and what was called "his transcendent Pure Land," his heavenly abode. Finally, especially among the ordinary people of China and Japan, there developed a widespread religious practice of invoking the Buddha under the title *Amida,* which comes from the Sanskrit word *amitabha,* meaning "immeasurable light." The Japanese version of this invocation is *Namu amida butsu.* It is thought that, by invoking the Buddha's name under this title in countless repetitions, one is assured of birth in the Pure Land, which is another way of saying one is assured of enlightenment.

What we see here is recognition of the power attached to a sacred name. The sacred scriptures of the Sikhs are also permeated by a sense of the power of God's name:

> Through belief in the Name
> the mind soars high into enlightenment,
> and the whole universe stands self-revealed.
> Through inner belief in the Name
> one avoids ignorant stumbling.
> In the light of such a faith
> the fear of death is broken.
> Such is the power of God's stainless Name.
> Those who truly believe in it, know it.[5]

For Christians, the most powerful and beautiful word is the name of Jesus all by itself, or some short phrase using the name of Jesus—"Jesus, have mercy," "O my Jesus," "Jesus, love" or the longer phrase passed on by the Eastern Christian tradition, "Lord Jesus Christ, Son of the Living God, have mercy on me," the Jesus Prayer. John Main taught (and now his student and friend Laurence Freeman continues to teach) people to use the Aramaic word *Maranatha.* The Greek form of this word is among the final words in the Book of Revelation, the last book of the New Testament. *Maranatha* means simply "Come, O Lord."

In the Roman tradition, at the end of the Advent season it is customary to sing the ancient and beautiful "O Antiphons." Named this way because each one begins with the invocation "O," these antiphons are used to introduce the chanting of the Canticle of Mary for evening prayer from December 17 to December 23. The

O Antiphons form the verses of the famous Advent hymn "O Come O Come Emmanuel," though most people only know that invocation, which is the last. The six other antiphons also use names for Jesus culled from scripture: O Wisdom, O Ruler of the House of Israel, O Root of Jesse, O Key of David, O Radiant Dawn, O King of All the Nations. What wonderful mantras any of these invocations would make.

The mantra is clearly important, as is commitment to the use of a single mantra. John Main is especially strict in his teaching about this, that we should not keep switching from mantra to mantra, that at some point we should settle into a word that is our own and trust it to lead us to the depths of our being. But at the same time this is not to say that we should ever be closed to a prayer word that wells up from out of our heart. There is a time for meditation proper but there is also a moment for walking down the street or doing any other ordinary action and suddenly seeing or hearing something that recalls God for us, and that gift becomes a word, and that word becomes a prayer, and that prayer leads us back into the silence of our hearts so that we can pray constantly and live prayerfully. All things are ultimately meant to lead us to the silence of our hearts; all things are meant to call to mind the steadfast love of God.

Conclusion

For me, what was so revolutionary about meditating—which I learned through Zen Buddhism and through Yoga, both of which brought me back to find my inspiration in the Gospel—was the discovery that my whole body, or more specifically my whole being, could be involved in prayer. Christians can sometimes give the impression that prayer involves leaving our bodies at the door, that everything about the body is at best suspect and at worst a hindrance to the spiritual life. This is astoundingly un-Christian, and especially counter to the liturgical/sacramental tradition of Roman Catholicism. The ancient patristic adage is that "the body is the instrument of salvation." Thus, all of me comes to prayer, all of me is reverenced in prayer, all of me can somehow be a tool, an instrument of prayer.

The goal of our spiritual life is our total transformation—body and soul—by God's Spirit. When we hear the story of Jesus' Transfiguration, we need to keep in mind what St. Paul says—that the Lord Jesus "will transform the body of our humiliation that it may be conformed to the body of his glory" (Phil 3:21). The body is meant to be transfigured by the Divine life; the mind, or the soul, is meant to participate in Divine consciousness—so St. Paul tells us: "Let the same mind be in you that was in Christ Jesus" (Phil 2:5). The spirit is meant to be totally open to God's Spirit, so that it becomes the place where we and God meet. What we celebrate at Christmas is actually what we celebrate at Pentecost: the Spirit descending into matter, impregnating matter. This is what Luke's Gospel focuses on, the descent. Then there is also a corresponding ascent, which is what John's Gospel focuses on.[6] The descent is "God's love [being] poured into our hearts through the Holy Spirit that has been given to us" (Rom 5:5). The ascent is matter being transformed by the indwelling power of the Spirit.

What the Christian believes is that ascent is what took place in Jesus' resurrection. In Jesus' body, matter has been transformed: Jesus' body of flesh has become a spiritual body, and through his spiritual body we are saved. We believe that by our contact with the Body of Christ, which is no longer limited by space or time, our human bodies have within them the seed of Divine life.[7] This is why St. Peter says, "You have been born anew, not of perishable but of imperishable seed, through the living and enduring word of God" (1 Pet 1:23).

That "living and enduring word of God" is the Word spoken of in the prologue to John's Gospel, the Word that was in the beginning, the Word through whom all things came into being, the Word that became flesh and lived among us (see John 1:1-18). The Word is the "Alpha and the Omega, the first and the last, the beginning and the end" (Rev 22:13).

This is why St. Paul says, "not only the creation, but we ourselves, who have the first fruits of the Spirit, groan inwardly while we wait for adoption, the redemption of our bodies" (Rom 8:23). As Fr. Bede Griffiths writes:

This groaning is the groaning of all creation which is waiting to be transfigured and delivered from its bondage to futility and decay and death. This is the cosmic drama—the transformation of nature, the transformation of matter and the body, so that all of nature, all matter, and our bodies may become outward manifestations of the divine Spirit.[8]

This is the transformation that is taking place in our own bodies. This is the real goal of all our meditative techniques and methods: the transformation of the body and soul by the power of the indwelling Spirit of God.

Let us end by meditating on this great mystery using the great word of Advent, the mantra taught by Fr. John Main, among the last words of all the words in our sacred scriptures: *Maranatha*! Come, O Lord!

POSTSCRIPT

I am finishing these chapters while staying at a small Christian ashram nestled above the Ganges in Rishikesh, in northern India. There are a few things that seem significant to me about working on this particular book here.

First of all, the ashram is in the village of Tapovan, which means the forest (*van*) of austerities (*tapas*). It has this name because, although now there is ever-expanding housing and a growing tourist-based economy here, there was a time when these hills were peopled with ascetics and Hindu renunciants devoted to their spiritual practices, to the search for knowledge of God.

Second, the ashram itself is named Jheevandhara Ashram, the ashram of "living water." This of course refers first of all to *Ganga-mata*, Mother Ganges, which flows below this place from one of the Himalayan sources of the sacred river. The "living water" also refers to John 7:37-38, words calligraphed on a wall here:

> Let all who are thirsty come to me; all who believe in me come and drink. Streams of living water shall flow from out of the believer's heart.

This is the first thing that catches the visitor's eye upon entering the gate of the ashram, and it struck me profoundly the first time I visited some years ago. It was the very verse that had initiated a radical change in my own life and had become for me the heart of the Gospel: Jesus himself telling us that as a result of his life, death, resurrection, and ascension there would be an outpouring of the Spirit of God directly into our hearts; that from then on we no longer would have to search for God "out there" but, by emptying ourselves in faith and sincerity, we could come to know the Spirit of God praying within us, the Spirit who is our union with God through, with, and in Jesus, and who will flow back out of our hearts to make glad the city of God in love and service.

Another significant thing about this setting is that this place, this Christian ashram, is a successful example of the incorporation of indigenous Indian spirituality, the native spiritual genius, in a Christian setting. This is seen not only in the outer elements—the use of gestures and symbols such as Sanskrit chants, art, and iconography—but also in practical spirituality as Indian sacred texts, "seeds of the word," the "cosmic revelation," are read and studied, and the specific interior focus of native Indian spirituality is exemplified by four hour-long periods of silent meditation each day. The foundress of this ashram, Sr. Vandana, and her successors, Srs. Ishpriya and Turiya, all sisters of the Congregation of the Sacred Heart, are also examples themselves of an embodiment of the best of the East and West, firmly rooted in Catholic Christianity, yet fully daughters of Mother India, bringing the wealth of nations to the feet of Jesus, the *sat-guru*, the light of all the nations.

The other significant thing for me is that several times here in Rishikesh I have heard from serious spiritual practitioners admonitions against people teaching before they themselves are ready, warnings about how often in Christianity we are so focused on the exterior, on missionary and apostolic work, at the expense of the interior, that there is a tendency to "give it before we live it." None of these folks knew that I was in the process of writing this book when they said these things, thus adding to the diffidence I was already feeling and always feel when daring to speak or write about prayer and meditation. The feelings grew deeper when, on at least two occasions, people speaking to me quoted the adage, "In the land of the blind, a one-eyed Jack becomes the King."

Not that you, kind reader, are blind, although I fear that perhaps in writing these pages I have been only a one-eyed Jack. Still, I hope there is a chance that—having written these chapters after many requests that I do so—instead of becoming your king, I have in fact been your servant, and that they will help you on your way, just as the wisdom contained herein, culled from many sources and sages, has helped and continues to help me, your brother on the way.

Cyprian Consiglio, OSB Cam.
6 February 2007
Jheevandhara Ashram, Tapovan, Rishikesh

GLOSSARY

asana	a body position assumed in yogic exercises
apatheia	a state of peace, of tranquility
apophatic theology	theology by way of negation
atman	the inner self that is one with Brahman
ashram	a usually secluded residence of a religious community and its guru
bija mantra	a "seed syllable" with no translatable meaning
Brahman	the Godhead beyond all name and form; the ground of being
chakras	according to yogic tradition, the seven energy centers in the body
dharana	concentration
dhikr	a Sufi practice signifying remembrance of God
dhyana	self-immersion; meditation
fana	a Sufi term meaning "the extinguishing of the ego," or complete absorption in God
half lotus position	a basic yogic cross-legged sitting position in which one foot is placed on the opposite thigh
hatha yoga	a branch of yoga that uses bodily postures, breathing techniques, and meditation to bring about a sound, healthy body and a clear, peaceful mind
hesychasm	tradition of inner mystical prayer associated with the monks of Mt. Athos in Greece
kerygma	proclamation, announcement, preaching

lotus position	a basic yogic cross-legged sitting position in which each foot is placed on the opposite thigh
mantra	a sacred word or sound used in meditation
OM	a sacred, untranslated syllable; the primal word; the Divine sound
perfect pose	a basic yogic cross-legged sitting position that brings the heels to the body
prana	vital force associated with breath
pranayama	control of the vital force by means of controlling the breath
rishi	a divinely inspired Hindu poet or sage; a seer
sadhana	a spiritual practice
samadhi	a Sanskrit term meaning absorption in the Divine, "enstasy" (a term coined in the late 1960s by Mircea Eliade to contrast the Eastern view of bliss as "standing inside oneself" with the Western view of bliss as "ecstasy," or "standing outside oneself")
sannyasi	a Hindu renunciant
shruti	a drone sound underlying Indian music
tasbih	Muslim beads used for prayer
vipassana	a Buddhist meditation technique
Vedas	sacred ancient texts of Hinduism
zazen	Zen meditation; literally, "seated meditation"
zendo	Zen meditation hall

Bibliography

Abhishiktananda. *The Further Shore*. Delhi: ISPCK, 1984.

———. *Guru and Disciple*. Delhi: ISPCK, 1974.

———. *Prayer*. Delhi: ISPCK, 1999.

Amaldas, Brahmachari. *Yoga and Contemplation*. Bangalore: Asian Trading Company, 2002.

The Art of Prayer: An Orthodox Anthology. Compiled by Igumen Chariton of Valmo. Translated by E. Kadloubovsky and E. M. Palmer. London: Faber and Faber, 1966.

Ascent to the Depth of the Heart: The Spiritual Diary of Abhishiktananda. Edited by Raimundo Pannikar. Translated by David Fleming and James Stuart. Dehli: ISPCK, 1998.

Aurobindo, Sri. *The Philosophy of the Upanishads*. Pondicherry: Sri Aurbindo Ashram Press, 1994.

———. *All India Magazine* (December 2006): 19–20.

Bhagavad Gita: the Song of God. Translated by Swami Prabhavananda and Christopher Isherwood, Introduction by Aldous Huxley. Hollywood, CA: Vedanta Press, 1987.

Bleichner, Howard P. *View from the Altar*. New York: Crossroad, 2004.

Bloom, Anthony. *Beginning to Pray*. New York: Paulist Press, 1970.

Burrows, Ruth. *Ascent to Love: The Spiritual Teaching of St. John of the Cross*. Denville, NJ: Dimension Books, 1987.

Campbell, Joseph. *Joseph Campbell and the Power of Myth with Bill Moyers*. DVD. Del Mar: Genius Products, 1988.

Catechism of the Catholic Church. English Translation ©1994 United States Catholic Conference, Inc. Citta del Vaticano: Libreria Editrice Vaticana, 1994.

Chetwynd, Tom. *Zen and the Kingdom of Heaven*. Boston: Wisdom Publications, 2001.

Christian Prayer: The Liturgy of the Hours. New York: Catholic Publishing Co., 1976.

Clement, Olivier, *The Roots of Christian Mysticism*. New York: New City Press, 1995.

The Cloud of Unknowing. Edited by William Johnston. Garden City: Image Books, 1973.

The Collected Works of St. John of the Cross. Translated by Kieran Kavanaugh and Otilio Rodriguez. Washington, DC: ICS Publications, 1991.

Congregation for the Doctrine of the Faith. "Letter to the Bishops of the Catholic Church on Some Aspects of Christian Meditation." Vatican City, 1989.

Consiglio, Cyprian, OSB Cam. "The Space in the Heart of the Lotus." Master's thesis, St. John's Seminary and School of Theology, 1997.

Dass, Ram. Liner notes. *The Chord of Love*. CD. Karuna, 2002.

de Caussade, Jean-Pierre. *Abandonment to Divine Providence*. Translated by John Beevers. New York: Image Books, 1975.

de Hueck Doherty, Catherine. *Poustinia*, Notre Dame: Ave Maria Press, 1975.

de Vogue, Adalert. *The Rule of Saint Benedict: A Doctrinal and Spiritual Commentary*. Kalamazoo, MI: Cistercian Publications, 1983.

Dechanet, J. M. *Christian Yoga*. Translated by Roland Hindmarsh. New York: Harper & Row Publishers, 1960.

Declaration on the Relations of the Church to Non-Christian Religions. *Nostra Aetate*. In *Vatican II: The Conciliar and Post Conciliar Documents*. Edited by Austin Flannery, OP. Northport, NY: Costello, 1992.

D'Silva, Russill Paul. "In the Beginning Was Music." In *The Other Half of My Soul: Bede Griffiths and the Hindu-Christian Dialogue*, compiled by Beatrice Bruteau, 64–78. Wheaton: Quest Books, 1996.

Dupuis, Jacques. *Gesú Cristo Incontro alle Religioni*. 2nd ed. Assisi: Cittadella Editrice, 1988.

Enomiya-Lassalle, Hugo M., SJ. *The Practice of Zen Meditation*. London: Aquarian Press, 1987.

Evdokimov, Paul. *The Sacrament of Love: The Nuptial Mystery in the Light of the Orthodox Tradition*. Translated by Anthony P. Gythiel and Victoria Stedman. Crestwood, NY: St. Vladimir's Press, 1985.

———. *Woman and the Salvation of the World: A Christian Anthropology on the Charisms of Woman*. Translated by Anthony P. Gythiel. Crestwood, NY: St. Vladimir's Press, 1994.

General Instruction of the Liturgy of the Hours, in *Christian Prayer: The Liturgy of the Hours*. New York: Catholic Publishing Co., 1976.

Griffiths, Bede. "Integration of Mind, Body, Spirit." *An Occasional Paper of the Fetzer Institute*. Kalamazoo, MI, 1994.

————. *New Creation in Christ.* Springfield, Templegate, 1992.

————. *A New Vision of Reality.* Springfield, Templegate, 1989.

————. "The 1989 Hibbert Lecture." *AIM Monastic Bulletin* 49 (1991): 51–58.

————. *Return to the Center.* Springfield: Templegate, 1976.

————. *River of Compassion: A Christian Commentary on the Bhagavad Gita.* New York: Continuum, 1995.

Gruen, Anselm. *Heaven Begins Within You: Wisdom from the Desert Fathers.* New York: Crossroad, 2000.

Guiver, George. *Company of Voices.* New York: Pueblo Publishing Company, 1988.

Henry, Gray, and Susannah Marriott. *Beads of Faith: Pathways to Meditation and Spirituality Using Rosaries, Prayer Beads, and Sacred Words.* Louisville: Fons Vita, 2008.

Jaffe, Lawrence. *Liberating the Heart: Spirituality and Jungian Psychology.* Toronto: Inner City Press, 1990.

John Cassian: The Conferences. Translated by Boniface Ramsey. New York: Newman Press, 1997.

John of the Cross. *The Ascent of Mount Carmel: The Collected Works of St. John of the Cross.* Translated by Kieran Kavanaugh and Otilio Rodriguez. Washington, DC: ICS Publications, 1991.

Johnston, William. *Arise, My Love: Mysticism for a New Era.* Maryknoll, NY: Orbis Books, 2000.

Jung, C. G. *Psychology and the East.* Princeton, NJ: Princeton University Press, 1978.

Kapleau, Philip. *The Three Pillars of Zen.* New York: Anchor Books, 1980.

Lao Tzu. *Tao Te Ching.* Translated by Gia-fu Feng and Jane English. New York: Vintage, 1989.

Legrand, L. "L'annonce a Marie." In *Letture dei Giorni.* Casale Monferrato: Edizioni Piemme, 1994.

Louf, André. *La Vita Spirituale.* Magnano: Edizioni Qiqajon, 2001.

Louth, Andrew. *The Origins of the Christian Mystical Tradition: From Plato to Denys.* Oxford: Clarendon Press, 1981.

Main, John. *Silence and Stillness in Every Season: Daily Readings with John Main.* Edited by Paul Harris. New York: Continuum, 1997.

Maloney, George. *The Breath of the Mystic.* Denville: Dimension Books, 1974.

Merton, Thomas. *The Hidden Ground of Love: The Letters of Thomas Merton on Religious Experience and Social Concerns.* New York: Farrar, Straus, and Giroux, 1985.

Muktananda, Swami. *Meditate: Happiness Lies Within You.* New York: SYDA Foundation, 1999.

Nanak, Guru. *Adi Granth.* In *The Sacred Writings of the Sikhs,* by K. Singh and George Sutherland Fraser, 27–119. Andhra Pradesh: Orient Blackswan, 2003.

The Office of Readings According to the Roman Rite. Boston: St. Paul Editions, 1983.

The One Light: Bede Griffiths' Principal Writings. Edited by Bruno Barnhart. Springfield: Templegate, 2001.

Oxford Dictionary of World Religions. Edited by John Bowker. New York: Oxford University Press, 1997.

Patanjali, Bhagwan Shree. *Aphorisms of Yoga.* Translated with commentary by Shree Purohit Swami. London: Faber and Faber Limited, 1938.

Paul, Russill. *The Yoga of Sound.* New York: The Relaxation Company, 2000.

The Quran. Translated by Abdullah Yusuf Ali. New York: Tahrike Tarsile Qur'an, Inc. 2001

Ramana Maharshi: A Short Life Sketch. Tiruvannamalai: Sri Ramanasram, 1995.

Rule of Saint Benedict. Edited by Timothy Fry. Collegeville, MN: Liturgical Press, 1981.

Sacred Texts of the World. Edited by Ninian Smart and Richard D. Hecht. New York: Crossroad, 1992.

Slade, Herbert. *Exploration into Contemplative Prayer.* New York: Paulist Press, 1975.

Smith, Cyprian. *The Way of Paradox: Spiritual Life as Taught by Meister Eckhart.* London: Darton, Longman & Todd, 1987.

Spidlik, Tomas. *The Spirituality of the Christian East: A Systematic Handbook.* Translated by Anthony P. Gythiel. Kalamazoo, MI: Cistercian Publications, 1986.

Suzuki, Shunryu. *Zen Mind, Beginner's Mind.* New York: Weatherhill, 1984.

Teachings of the Buddha. Edited by Jack Kornfield. Boston: Shambala, 1996.

Universal Wisdom: A Journey through the Sacred Wisdom of the World. Selected and introduced by Bede Griffiths. London: HarperCollins, 1994.

Vannini, Marco. *L'esperienza dello Spirito.* Palermo: Edizioni Augustinus, 1991.

Ware, Kallistos. *The Power of the Name.* Oxford: SLG Press, 1974.

Wilber, Ken. *Kosmic Konsciousness.* CD. Boulder: Sounds True, 2003.

Williams, Rowan. *Writing in the Dust: After September 11.* Grand Rapids: Wm. B. Eerdmans, 2002.

The Wisdom of Teresa of Avila: *Selections from the Interior Castle.* Edited by Stephen J. Connor. Translated by Kieran Kavanaugh and Otilio Rodriguez. New York: Paulist Press, 1979.

The Wound of Love: A Carthusian Miscellany. Kalamazoo, MI: Cistercian Publications, 1994.

Writings from the Philokalia: On Prayer of the Heart. Translated by E. Kadloubovsky and G. H. E. Palmer. Compiled by St. Nicodemus of the Holy Mountain and St. Makarios of Corinth. London: Faber & Faber, 1992.

Zepp, Ira G., Jr. *A Muslim Primer: Beginner's Guide to Islam.* Westminster: Wakefield Editions, 1992.

NOTES

Preface, pages vii–xi

1. Abhishiktananda, *The Further Shore* (Delhi: ISPCK, 1984) 9; line breaks are mine.

Chapter 1, pages 1–18

1. *Katha Upanishad*, II.I.1; unless otherwise noted, all quotes from non–Judeo-Christian scriptures are my own poetic adaptations from various translations.

2. In classical form, the *sannyasi* is a wanderer and a beggar, one who has gone beyond all ritual and activity. Both Abhishiktananda and Bede Griffiths considered *sannyasi* to be the equivalent of the essence of Christian monasticism as well.

3. Quoted in Tomas Spidlik, *The Spirituality of the Christian East: A Systematic Handbook*, trans. Anthony P. Gythiel (Kalamazoo, MI: Cistercian Publications, 1986) 88.

4. C. G. Jung, *Psychology and the East* (Princeton, NJ: Princeton University Press, 1978) 160.

5. Bede Griffiths, *Return to the Center* (Springfield: Templegate, 1976) 71–75.

6. Lawrence Jaffe, *Liberating the Heart: Spirituality and Jungian Psychology* (Toronto: Inner City Press, 1990) 23.

7. William Johnston, *Arise, My Love: Mysticism for a New Era* (Maryknoll, NY: Orbis Books, 2000) 40. An important side note: William Johnston notes that "to Christians living in Asia it becomes increasingly clear that inter-religious dialogue must be carried on principally at the level of mysticism," because the mysticism of Hinduism, Buddhism, and Taoism has so penetrated Asian culture that they "live in the unconscious of the people," and influence their "way of thinking and feeling and acting, influencing art and architecture, literature and poetry." Bede Griffiths adds, "I have to be a Hindu, a Buddhist, a Jain, a Parsee, a Sikh, a Muslim, and a Jew, as well as a Christian, if I am to know the Truth and to find the point of reconciliation in all religion" (*Return to the Center*, 71–75).

8. Bede Griffiths, *River of Compassion: A Christian Commentary on the Bhagavad Gita* (New York: Continuum, 1995) 130.

9. Ibid.

10. Congregation for the Doctrine of the Faith, "Letter to the Bishops of the Catholic Church on Some Aspects of Christian Meditation" (Vatican City, 1989) no. 16.

11. Declaration on the Relations of the Church to Non-Christian Religions. *Nostra Aetate*, no. 2, in *Vatican II: The Conciliar and Post Conciliar Documents*, ed. Austin Flannery, OP (Northport, NY: Costello, 1992).

12. Congregation for the Doctrine of the Faith, "Letter to the Bishops," no. 16.

13. For example, the *Catechism of the Catholic Church* says: "Sometimes the soul is distinguished from the spirit . . . This distinction does not introduce a duality into the soul. 'Spirit' signifies that from creation [human beings are] ordered to a supernatural end and that [one's] soul can be gratuitously raised . . . to communion with God." *Catechism of the Catholic Church*, English translation, United States Catholic Conference, Inc. (Citta del Vaticano: Libreria Editrice Vaticana, 1994) no. 367.

14. Bede Griffiths, "The 1989 Hibbert Lecture," *AIM Monastic Bulletin* 49 (1991) 51–58.

15. Marco Vannini, *L'Esperienza dello Spirito* (Palermo: Edizioni Augustinus, 1991) 41.

16. Bede Griffiths, "Integration of Mind, Body, Spirit," *An Occasional Paper of the Fetzer Institute* (Kalamazoo, MI: 1994) 1.

17. Ken Wilber, *Kosmic Konsciousness*, CD (Boulder, CO: Sounds True, 2003) disc 8, part 6.

18. Vannini, *L'Esperienza dello Spirito*, 41.

19. Ibid.

20. Swami Muktananda, *Meditate: Happiness Lies Within You* (New York: SYDA Foundation, 1999) 27.

21. Philip Kapleau, *The Three Pillars of Zen* (New York: Anchor Books, 1980) 35.

22. Hugo M. Enomiya-Lassalle, SJ, *The Practice of Zen Meditation* (London: Aquarian Press, 1987) 17.

Chapter 2, pages 19–29

1. Bede Griffiths, *River of Compassion: A Christian Commentary on the Bhagavad Gita* (New York: Continuum, 1995) 273.

2. See also Matthew 14:23, Mark 6:46, Luke 5:16, and Luke 9:28.

3. *The Art of Prayer: An Orthodox Anthology*, comp. Igumen Chariton of Valmo, trans. E. Kadloubovsky and E. M. Palmer (London: Faber and Faber, 1966) 45–46.

4. St. Benedict in his rule for monks also uses the Lord's Prayer in the context of forgiveness: "The Morning and Evening Office must certainly not pass without the Lord's Prayer being said at the end in its place by the Superior

for all to hear, because of the thorns of scandal that are wont to spring up. Thus warned by the agreement made in that prayer when they say 'Forgive us as we forgive,' the brethren may clear themselves of this kind of fault." *Rule of Saint Benedict*, ed. Timothy Fry (Collegeville, MN: Liturgical Press, 1981) ch. 13.

5. In the Gospel of Matthew alone we can find many such cases. See, for example, Matthew 8:13, 9:22, 9:29, and 15:28.

6. This, by the way, is the text of the antiphon used in the Roman Rite for Pentecost day, the day on which we celebrate the coming of the Holy Spirit.

7. *Chandogya Upanishad*, VIII.I.1.

8. *Writings from the Philokalia: On Prayer of the Heart*, trans. E. Kadloubovsky and G. H. E. Palmer, comp. St. Nicodemus of the Holy Mountain and St. Makarios of Corinth (London: Faber & Faber, 1992) 30.

9. See Matthew 13:44-46.

10. Jean-Pierre de Caussade, *Abandonment to Divine Providence*, trans. John Beevers (New York: Image Books, 1975) 25–26.

11. *Chandogya Upanishad*, III.XIV.2–3.

12. Quoted in Tomas Spidlik, *The Spirituality of the Christian East: A Systematic Handbook*, trans. Anthony P. Gythiel (Kalamazoo: Cistercian Publications, 1986) 61.

13. *The Cloud of Unknowing*, ed. William Johnston (Garden City: Image Books, 1973) 95–96.

14. Ibid.

Chapter 3, pages 30–42

1. Bede Griffiths, *A New Vision of Reality* (Springfield: Templegate, 1989) 97.

2. Jacques Dupuis, *Gesù Cristo Incontro alle Religioni*, 2nd ed. (Assisi: Cittadella Editrice, 1988) 154–55.

3. Paul Evdokimov, *Woman and the Salvation of the World: A Christian Anthropology on the Charisms of Woman*, trans. Anthony P. Gythiel (Crestwood, NY: St. Vladimir's Press, 1994) 39.

4. Paul Evdokimov, *The Sacrament of Love: The Nuptial Mystery in the Light of the Orthodox Tradition*, trans. Anthony P. Gythiel and Victoria Stedman (Crestwood, NY: St. Vladimir's Press, 1985) 51.

5. Cyprian Consiglio, OSB Cam, "The Space in the Heart of the Lotus" (master's thesis, St. John's Seminary and School of Theology, 1997) 27.

6. Tomas Spidlik, *The Spirituality of the Christian East: A Systematic Handbook*, trans. Anthony P. Gythiel (Kalamazoo, MI: Cistercian Publications, 1986) 92. Spidlik does admit that some confusion in terms may be noted. He himself vacillates between upper case and lower case "s" for "Spirit," as in the human spirit versus the Holy Spirit. See his chapter 4, "Christian Anthropology" for an excellent treatment, especially in the section titled "Various Aspects of the Trichotomy."

7. Howard P. Bleichner, *View from the Altar* (New York: Crossroad, 2004) 76.

8. *The Quran*, trans. Abdullah Yusuf Ali (New York: Tahrike Tarsile Qur'an, Inc. 2001) Surah 50:16.

9. From the *Confessions of Saint Augustine* (10.27.38, 10.10.16), quoted in *The Office of Readings According to the Roman Rite* (Boston: St. Paul Editions, 1983) 1537–38.

10. Bleichner, *View from the Altar*, 76.

11. From the Jain *Nityanaimittika-pathavali*, in *Sacred Texts of the World*, ed. Ninian Smart and Richard D. Hecht (New York: Crossroad, 1992) 287.

12. Anthony Bloom, *Beginning to Pray* (New York: Paulist Press, 1970) 46.

13. John Main, *Silence and Stillness in Every Season: Daily Readings with John Main*, ed. Paul Harris (New York: Continuum, 1997) 253.

14. Ibid., 254.

15. Cyprian Smith, *The Way of Paradox: Spiritual Life as Taught by Meister Eckhart* (London: Darton, Longman & Todd, 1987) 12.

16. Ibid.

17. Ibid., 12–13.

18. Those familiar with the yogic tradition may be aware of the teaching that the body has seven energy centers called *chakras*. Each one of these *chakras* is associated with a *bija* mantra: *lam-vam-ram-yam-hum-OM*. Note that there are only six *bija* mantras listed here; the seventh *chakra*, which is at the crown of the head, has no sound.

19. Some modern scholars think that this mantra may actually be a corruption of a Sanskrit mantra, and that it is actually an invocation to a female deity named *Manipadma*, surrounded by two syllables "*OM*" and "*hum*," both of which are *bija* or "seed" syllables.

20. *Oxford Dictionary of World Religions*, ed. John Bowker (New York: Oxford University Press, 1997) 714. The author of the entry in the *Oxford Dictionary* explains the complicated etymology of this mantra, and seems at pains to inform us that most translations are misconceived, with even this understanding being a paraphrase at best.

Chapter 4, pages 43–54

1. *General Instruction of the Liturgy of the Hours*, #9, in *Christian Prayer: The Liturgy of the Hours* (New York: Catholic Publishing Co., 1976) 13.

2. Adalbert de Vogue, *The Rule of Saint Benedict: A Doctrinal and Spiritual Commentary* (Kalamazoo, MI: Cistercian Publications, 1983) 129.

3. From the *Life of Saint Antony* by Saint Athanasius (Cap. 2–4), quoted in *The Office of Readings According to the Roman Rite* (Boston: St. Paul Editions, 1983) 1309.

4. From the earliest days of Christianity there were some members of the church who were more committed than the majority, who wished to live a life of particular asceticism and commitment, even to the extent of renouncing marriage and family ties: the order of virgins and celibates. These came to be

known by various names such as *devoti*, the devout. By the third and fourth centuries such *devoti*, although continuing to worship in the local church, were beginning to live in community and to develop strong liturgical characteristics of their own, especially in Syria.

5. George Guiver, *Company of Voices* (New York: Pueblo Publishing Company, 1988) 54.

6. *John Cassian: The Conferences*, trans. Boniface Ramsey (New York: Newman Press, 1997) 379; line breaks are mine.

7. Ibid., 381–82.

8. Shunryu Suzuki, *Zen Mind, Beginner's Mind* (New York: Weatherhill, 1984) 34.

9. From the *Sutta-Nipata*, trans. Dines Anderson and Helmer Smith, quoted in *Teachings of the Buddha*, ed. Jack Kornfield (Boston: Shambala, 1996) 79.

10. Kallistos Ware, *The Power of the Name* (Oxford: SLG Press, 1974) 13.

11. *Universal Wisdom: A Journey through the Sacred Wisdom of the World*, selected and introduced by Bede Griffiths (London: HarperCollins, 1994) 244.

12. John Main, *Silence and Stillness in Every Season: Daily Readings with John Main*, ed. Paul Harris (New York: Continuum, 1997) 206.

13. Ibid., 206.

14. *Ramana Maharshi: A Short Life Sketch* (Tiruvannamalai: Sri Ramanasram, 1995) 2.

15. Philip Kapleau, *The Three Pillars of Zen* (New York: Anchor Books, 1980) 342.

16. Ibid.

Chapter 5, pages 55–68

1. *John Cassian: The Conferences*, trans. Boniface Ramsey (New York: Newman Press, 1997) 379.

2. Tom Chetwynd, *Zen and the Kingdom of Heaven* (Boston: Wisdom Publications, 2001) 77.

3. *Oxford Dictionary of World Religions*, ed. John Bowker (New York: Oxford University Press, 1997) 81.

4. Cyprian Smith, *The Way of Paradox: Spiritual Life as Taught by Meister Eckhart* (London: Darton, Longman and Todd, 1987) 35–36.

5. Gregory of Nyssa, *Commentary on the Song* XI: 1000–1, quoted in Andrew Louth, *The Origins of the Christian Mystical Tradition: From Plato to Denys* (Oxford: Clarendon Press, 1981) 83.

6. Ibid.

7. From the *Journey of the Mind to God* by Saint Bonaventure (Cap. 7, 4. 6: *Opera omnia* 5, 312–313), quoted in *The Office of Readings According to the Roman Rite* (Boston: St. Paul Editions, 1983) 1474–75.

8. *John Cassian: The Conferences*, 383.

9. Ira G. Zepp, Jr., *A Muslim Primer: Beginner's Guide to Islam* (Westminster: Wakefield Editions, 1992) 164.

10. Thomas Merton, *The Hidden Ground of Love: The Letters of Thomas Merton on Religious Experience and Social Concerns* (New York: Farrar, Straus, and Giroux, 1985) 63–64.

11. Sri Aurobindo, *The Philosophy of the Upanishads* (Pondicherry: Sri Aurbindo Ashram Press, 1994) 30.

12. Catherine de Hueck Doherty, *Poustinia* (Notre Dame: Ave Maria Press, 1975) 130–31.

13. *Brihadaranyaka Upanishad,* IV.II.4.

14. Sri Aurobindo, *The Philosophy of the Upanishads,* 18–19.

15. "Praise for you is silence" (Ps 65:1). Abhishiktananda, *Prayer* (Delhi: ISPCK, 1999) 81–82.

16. *The Wound of Love: A Carthusian Miscellany* (Kalamazoo, MI: Cistercian Publications, 1994) 123–24; line breaks are mine.

17. Rowan Williams, *Writing in the Dust: After September 11* (Grand Rapids: Wm. B. Eerdmans, 2002) 3.

18. Paul Evdokimov, *Woman and the Salvation of the World: A Christian Anthropology on the Charisms of Woman,* trans. Anthony P. Gythiel (Crestwood, NY: St. Vladimir's Press, 1994) 43.

19. Russill Paul D'Silva, "In the Beginning Was Music," in *The Other Half of My Soul: Bede Griffiths and the Hindu-Christian Dialogue,* comp. Beatrice Bruteau (Wheaton: Quest Books, 1996) 65.

20. See Herbert Slade's paraphrased extracts from the Yoga Sutras with explanations in *Exploration into Contemplative Prayer* (New York: Paulist Press, 1975) 209–10.

21. "Commentary on No. 27," *Aphorisms of Yoga,* by Bhagwan Shree Patanjali, trans. with commentary by Shree Purohit Swami (London: Faber and Faber Limited, 1938) 38.

22. Abhishiktananda, *Prayer* (Delhi: ISPCK, 1999) 112.

23. *Ascent to the Depth of the Heart: The Spiritual Diary of Abhishiktananda,* ed. Raimundo Pannikar, trans. David Fleming and James Stuart (Dehli: ISPCK, 1998) 166.

24. Ibid.

25. Ibid., 112.

26. This is how Russill Paul has it in the extensive notes that accompany his CD *Shabda Yoga,* from his collection *The Yoga of Sound* (New York: The Relaxation Company, 2000) 8. See also the *Mundaka Upanishad* II.2.4: "The Om is the bow, the arrow the self: Brahman is the target, it is said."

27. Joseph Campbell, *Joseph Campbell and the Power of Myth with Bill Moyers* (Del Mar: Genius Products, 1988) DVD, session 4.

Chapter 6, pages 69–82

1. Andrew Louth, *The Origins of the Christian Mystical Tradition: From Plato to Denys* (Oxford: Clarendon Press, 1981) 53.

2. Ibid., 58.

3. Ibid., 57.

4. *The Wisdom of Teresa of Avila: Selections from the Interior Castle*, ed. Stephen J. Connor, trans. Kieran Kavanaugh and Otilio Rodriguez (New York: Paulist Press, 1979) 53.

5. Ibid., 58.

6. Sri Aurobindo, quoted in *All India Magazine* (December 2006) 19–20.

7. Quoted in Olivier Clement, *The Roots of Christian Mysticism* (New York: New City Press, 1995) 22.

8. Ibid.

9. Bede Griffiths, *New Creation in Christ* (Springfield, Templegate, 1992) 42.

10. Lao Tzu, *Tao Te Ching*, trans. Gia-fu Feng and Jane English (New York: Vintage, 1989) p. 3.

11. Space does not permit us to do justice here to this great and influential teacher. For those seeking to learn more about Evagrius of Pontus, I would recommend Anselm Gruen's book, *Heaven Begins Within You: Wisdom from the Desert Fathers* (New York: Crossroad, 2000). I am also omitting discussion of the important influence of Pseudo-Dionysius, whose foundational writings on the theme of the three stages are also worth pursuing.

12. Henri J. Nouwen, *The Inner Voice of Love: A Journey Through Anguish to Freedom* (New York: Image Books, 1996) 21.

13. John of the Cross, *The Ascent of Mount Carmel: The Collected Works of St. John of the Cross*, trans. Kieran Kavanaugh and Otilio Rodriguez (Washington, D.C.: ICS Publications, 1991) II.4.2.

14. Ibid.

15. Ruth Burrows, *Ascent to Love: The Spiritual Teaching of St. John of the Cross* (Denville, NJ: Dimension Books, 1987) 77.

16. Abhishiktananda warns that we Westerners too often let ourselves be beguiled by interior experiences, which make us think we have reached the summit. "Then we live in a pseudo-spiritual world where our ego becomes swollen, without our realizing it, under the cover of wonderful formulas of *emptiness* and *nothingness*. From the heights of our aristocratic, esoteric experience we mercilessly judge others who are still occupied on the inferior level of rites and myths, quite unaware of the fact that we ourselves are living in a myth which is infinitely more harmful than the one we are denouncing in others" (*Guru and Disciple* [Delhi: ISPCK, 1974] 12).

17. Sri Aurobindo, quoted in *All India Magazine* (December 2006) 19–20.

18. Ibid.

19. Brahmachari Amaldas, *Yoga and Contemplation* (Bangalore, Asian Trading Company, 2002) 24–25.

Chapter 7, pages 83–93

1. Tomas Spidlik says that "the philosophical dichotomy (body-soul) had to be completed by a theological trichotomy (body, soul, Spirit), which became traditional in the East," although he admits that a "certain confusion in the

use and meaning of the terms may be noted," especially with regard to what to call this third element. See his excellent treatment in *The Spirituality of the Christian East: A Systematic Handbook*, trans. Anthony P. Gythiel (Kalamazoo, MI: Cistercian Publications, 1986) ch. 4; quote above is from p. 92.

2. Theophan the Recluse, in *The Art of Prayer: An Orthodox Anthology*, comp. Igumen Chariton of Valmo, trans. E. Kadloubovsky and E. M. Palmer (London: Faber and Faber, 1966) 60–61.

3. Spidlik, *The Spirituality of the Christian East*, 103.

4. Kallistos Ware, "Introduction," *The Art of Prayer*, 18.

5. Ibid., 19.

6. Theophan the Recluse, in *The Art of Prayer*, 190.

7. Ibid., 191.

8. Kallistos Ware, *The Power of the Name* (Oxford: SLG Press, 1974) 18.

9. Theophan the Recluse, in *The Art of Prayer*, 52, 63.

10. Ibid., 52.

11. Ibid.

12. Ibid., 67.

13. Ibid., 22.

14. *Bhagavad Gita: The Song of God*, trans. Swami Prabhavananda and Christopher Isherwood, introduction by Aldous Huxley (Hollywood, CA: Vedanta Press, 1987) 8:12-13

15. Bede Griffiths, *River of Compassion: A Christian Commentary on the Bhagavad Gita* (New York: Continuum, 1995) 154.

16. Gray Henry and Susannah Marriott, *Beads of Faith: Pathways to Meditation and Spirituality Using Rosaries, Prayer Beads, and Sacred Words* (Louisville: Fons Vita, 2008) 95.

17. Ira G. Zepp, Jr., *A Muslim Primer: Beginner's Guide to Islam* (Westminster: Wakefield Editions, 1992) 163.

18. Al Ghazali, "Deliverance from Error," trans. Montgomery Watt, in *Universal Wisdom: A Journey through the Sacred Wisdom of the World*, selected and introduced by Bede Griffiths (London: HarperCollins, 1994) 345.

19. S. Bikram-Shah, "Le Yoga, ses exercices, son but et ses effets," quoted in J. M. Dechanet, *Christian Yoga*, trans. Roland Hindmarsh (New York: Harper & Row Publishers, 1960) 32.

20. Simeon the New Theologian, in *Writings from the Philokalia: On Prayer of the Heart*, trans. E. Kadloubovsky and G. H. E. Palmer, comp. St. Nicodemus of the Holy Mountain and St. Makarios of Corinth (London: Faber & Faber, 1992) 132.

21. Nicephorus the Solitary, "Profitable Discourse on Sobriety," in *Writings from the Philokalia*, 33.

Chapter 8, pages 94–104

1. André Louf, *La Vita Spirituale* (Magnano: Edizioni Qiqajon, 2001) 85–86 (my translation).

2. Gray Henry and Susannah Marriott, *Beads of Faith: Pathways to Meditation and Spirituality Using Rosaries, Prayer Beads, and Sacred Words* (Louisville: Fons Vita, 2008) 94.

3. George Maloney, *The Breath of the Mystic* (Denville: Dimension Books, 1974) 162.

4. Ram Dass, CD liner notes, *The Chord of Love* (Karuna, 2002).

5. Guru Nanak, *Adi Granth*, in *The Sacred Writings of the Sikhs*, by K. Singh and George Sutherland Fraser (Andhra Pradesh: Orient Blackswan, 2003) 35.

6. L. Legrand, "L'annonce a Marie," in *Letture dei Giorni. (*Casale Monferrato: Edizioni Piemme, 1994) 55.

7. Bede Griffiths, *Return to the Center* (Springfield: Templegate, 1976) 139.

8. Ibid.